THE AUSTRALIAN
Women's Weekly
classic.retro
recipes

acp
books

contents

The oven temperatures in this book are for conventional ovens; if you have a fan-forced oven, decrease the temperature by 10-20 degrees. A measurement conversion chart appears on the back flap of this book.

at the milk bar

spiders

8 scoops (480ml) vanilla ice-cream
1.25 litres (5 cups) creaming soda

1 Place two scoops of ice-cream in each of four 1½-cup (375ml) glasses; top with creaming soda.

prep time 5 minutes **serves** 4
nutritional count per serving
6.4g total fat (4.2g saturated fat); 970kJ (232 cal); 43.8g carbohydrate; 2.1g protein; 0g fibre

tip We used creaming soda but you can use any fizzy drink you like. Lemonade, cola, ginger beer, lime or orange would work just as well.

spiced
iced coffee
milkshake

¼ cup (20g) ground espresso coffee

¾ cup (180ml) boiling water

2 cardamom pods, bruised

¼ teaspoon ground cinnamon

1 tablespoon brown sugar

3 scoops (375ml) low-fat vanilla
ice-cream

2½ cups (625ml) no-fat milk

1 Place coffee then the water
in coffee plunger; stand 2 minutes
before plunging. Pour coffee into
small heatproof bowl with cardamom,
cinnamon and sugar; stir to dissolve
sugar then cool 10 minutes.
2 Strain coffee mixture through fine
sieve into blender or processor; add
ice-cream and milk, blend until
smooth. Serve immediately.

prep time 5 minutes
makes 1 litre (4 cups)
nutritional count per 250ml
1.6g fat (1.1g saturated fat);
500kJ (119 cal);
18g carbohydrate;
8.6g protein; 0.8g fibre

strawberry milkshake

200g (6½ ounces) frozen low-fat
  strawberry yogurt

250g (8 ounces) strawberries

1 litre (4 cups) milk

1 Soften yogurt slightly; cut into pieces. Hull strawberries; cut in half.
2 Blend or process yogurt, berries and milk until smooth.

prep time 10 minutes serves 4
nutritional count per serving
10.7g total fat (7g saturated fat);
1012kJ (242 cal);
24.7g carbohydrate;
12.2g protein; 1.4g fibre

curried egg sandwiches

corned beef and pickle sandwiches

curried egg sandwiches

6 eggs

⅓ cup (100g) mayonnaise

2 teaspoons curry powder

2 cups shredded iceberg lettuce

8 slices white bread (360g)

1 Cook eggs in large saucepan of boiling water about 7 minutes or until hard. Drain under cold water, then peel and chop egg coarsely.
2 Use a fork to mash egg, mayonnaise and curry powder in medium bowl; season to taste.
3 Sandwich egg mixture and lettuce between bread slices. Cut crusts from bread; cut each sandwich into four triangles to serve.

prep + cook time 30 minutes
makes 16 triangles
nutritional count per triangle
4.6g total fat (1g saturated fat); 448kJ (107 cal); 11.5g carbohydrate; 4.5g protein; 0.9g fibre

corned beef and pickle sandwiches

8 slices wholemeal bread (360g)

40g (1½ ounces) butter, softened

4 tablespoons mustard pickles

8 slices corned beef (240g)

1 Spread bread with butter; spread pickles on four slices. Top pickles with corned beef, season. Top with remaining bread. Cut in half diagonally to serve.

prep time 15 minutes **makes** 4
nutritional count per sandwich
14.8g total fat (7.5g saturated fat); 1574kJ (376 cal); 38g carbohydrate; 19.5g protein; 6g fibre

cheeseburgers with caramelised onion

500g (1 pound) minced (ground) beef

4 thin slices cheddar cheese (40g)

4 hamburger buns, split

8 large butter (boston) lettuce leaves

1 small tomato (90g), sliced thinly

4 large dill pickles (240g), sliced thinly

1 tablespoon american-style mustard

⅓ cup (95g) tomato sauce (ketchup)

caramelised onion

2 tablespoons olive oil

2 medium white onions (300g), sliced thinly

1 tablespoon light brown sugar

2 tablespoons balsamic vinegar

2 tablespoons water

1 Make caramelised onion.

2 Shape beef into four patties; cook on heated oiled grill plate (or grill or barbecue) until cooked through. Top each patty with cheese slices during last minute of cooking time.

3 Meanwhile, toast buns, cut-sides down, on grill plate.

4 Sandwich lettuce, tomato, patties, pickle and onion between buns; serve with mustard and tomato sauce.

CARAMELISED ONION Heat oil in large frying pan; cook onion, stirring, until soft. Add sugar, vinegar and the water; cook, stirring, until onion is caramelised.

prep + cook time 55 minutes
serves 4
nutritional count per serving
23.6g total fat (7.4g saturated fat); 2378kJ (569 cal); 51.6g carbohydrate; 34.9g protein; 5g fibre

corn and goat's cheese quesadillas

2 corn cobs (800g), trimmed

240g (7½ ounces) soft goat's cheese

8 large (20cm/8-inch) flour tortillas

½ cup (100g) char-grilled capsicum (bell pepper), sliced thinly

40g (1½ ounces) jalapeño chilli slices, drained

⅓ cup coarsely chopped fresh coriander (cilantro)

20g (¾ ounce) butter

40g (1½ ounces) baby spinach leaves

1 lime, cut into wedges

1 Cook corn on heated oiled grill plate (or grill or barbecue) until kernels are tender and browned lightly; when cool enough to handle, cut kernels from cobs.

2 Spread cheese over tortillas. Top four of the tortillas with corn, capsicum, chilli and coriander; season. Top with remaining tortillas; press around edges firmly to seal quesadillas.

3 Heat butter in medium frying pan; cook quesadillas, one at a time, until browned both sides and heated through.

4 Serve quesadillas with spinach and lime wedges.

prep + cook time 30 minutes
serves 4
nutritional count per serving
21.7g total fat
(10g saturated fat); 2169kJ
(519 cal); 57g carbohydrate;
19.8g protein; 8.6g fibre

tip A quesadilla (from 'queso', the Spanish word for cheese) is a tortilla 'sandwich' containing cheese and any number of spicy filling ingredients. It is grilled, fried or toasted and usually served with salsa.

banana split

1 cup (250ml) thickened (heavy) cream

4 medium bananas (800g), halved lengthways

4 scoops (240ml) chocolate ice-cream

4 scoops (240ml) vanilla ice-cream

4 scoops (240ml) strawberry ice-cream

4 maraschino cherries

1 tablespoon hundreds and thousands (nonpareils)

1 Beat cream in small bowl with electric mixer until firm peaks form. Spoon mixture into piping bag fitted with large fluted nozzle.

2 Place two banana halves in each of four dishes; place a scoop of chocolate, vanilla and strawberry ice-cream between banana halves in each dish.

3 Pipe cream on top of each ice-cream scoop, then top with cherries and sprinkle with hundreds and thousands.

prep time 20 minutes **serves** 4
nutritional count per serving
33.3g total fat
(21.8g saturated fat); 2236kJ
(535 cal); 53.6g carbohydrate;
6.9g protein; 3g fibre

apple cranberry pie

2 cups (300g) plain (all-purpose) flour

150g (4½ ounces) cold unsalted butter, chopped coarsely

¼ cup (60ml) iced water, approximately

1 egg

1 tablespoon milk

1 tablespoon caster (superfine) sugar

cranberry filling

½ cup (110g) caster (superfine) sugar

2 tablespoons water

300g (9½ ounces) frozen cranberries

apple filling

10 medium apples (1.5kg)

½ cup (125ml) water

⅓ cup (75g) caster (superfine) sugar

1 Process flour and butter until crumbly. With motor operating, add enough of the water to make ingredients come together. Turn dough onto floured surface, knead gently until smooth. Wrap pastry in plastic; refrigerate 1 hour.
2 Make cranberry filling. Make apple filling.
3 Preheat oven to 220°C/400°F.
4 Divide pastry in half. Roll half between sheets of baking paper until large enough to line deep 25cm (10-inch) pie dish. Lift pastry into pan; press over base and side, trim excess pastry. Prick base all over with fork.
5 Spoon cranberry filling into pastry case; top with apple filling. Brush pastry edge with combined egg and milk.
6 Roll remaining pastry until large enough to cover top of pie; press edges together with fork to seal. Brush with egg mixture; sprinkle with sugar.
7 Bake pie 15 minutes. Reduce oven temperature to 180°C/350°F; bake about 30 minutes.

CRANBERRY FILLING Combine sugar, the water and cranberries in medium saucepan; simmer, stirring, about 10 minutes or until syrupy. Remove from heat; cool.

APPLE FILLING Peel, quarter, core and slice apples thinly; combine in large saucepan with the water. Simmer, stirring occasionally, about 10 minutes or until apple is tender. Drain apple; discard liquid. Stir sugar into apple; cool.

prep + cook time 1¾ hours (+ refrigeration) serves 8
nutritional count per serving 16.8g total fat (10.5g saturated fat); 1981kJ (474 cal); 72.2g carbohydrate; 5.7g protein; 4.9g fibre

tip Both granny smith and golden delicious apples are suitable for this recipe.

time for tea

sultana and lemon scones

2½ cups (375g) self-raising flour

1 tablespoon caster (superfine) sugar

¼ teaspoon salt

30g (1 ounce) butter

½ cup (80g) sultanas

2 teaspoons grated lemon rind

¾ cup (180ml) milk

½ cup (125ml) water, approximately

1 Preheat oven to 240°C/475°F. Grease deep 19cm (8-inch) square cake pan.
2 Place flour, sugar and salt in large bowl; rub in butter with fingertips. Stir in the sultanas and rind.
3 Make a well in the centre of the flour mixture; add milk and almost all of the water. Using a knife, cut the milk and water through the flour mixture to mix to a soft, sticky dough. Add the remaining water only if needed for correct consistency.

4 Knead dough quickly and lightly on floured surface until smooth. Press dough out evenly to 2cm (¾-inch) thickness. Dip 4.5cm (1¾-inch) round cutter into flour; cut as many rounds as you can from the piece of dough.
5 Place scones side by side, just touching, in pan. Gently knead scraps of dough together; repeat pressing and cutting out of dough. Place rounds in pan; brush tops with a little extra milk.
6 Bake scones about 15 minutes.

prep + cook time 35 minutes **makes** 16
nutritional count per scone
2.3g total fat (1.3g saturated fat); 510kJ (122 cal); 21.9g carbohydrate; 2.8g protein; 1.1g fibre

tip Scones should be browned and sound hollow when tapped firmly on the top with your fingers. The scones in the middle are the ones to tap, as they will take the longest to cook.

serving suggestion Butter and jam or lemon curd.

mini chicken and leek pies

1 cup (250ml) chicken stock

170g (5½ ounces) chicken breast fillet

1 tablespoon olive oil

1 small leek (200g), sliced thinly

½ stalk celery (75g), chopped finely

2 teaspoons plain (all-purpose) flour

2 teaspoons fresh thyme leaves

¼ cup (60ml) pouring cream

1 teaspoon wholegrain mustard

2 sheets shortcrust pastry

1 sheet puff pastry

1 egg yolk

2 teaspoons sesame seeds

1 Bring stock to the boil in small saucepan. Add chicken; return to the boil. Reduce heat; simmer, covered, about 10 minutes or until chicken is cooked through. Remove from heat; stand chicken in poaching liquid 10 minutes. Remove chicken; chop finely. Reserve ¼ cup of the poaching liquid; discard remainder.

2 Heat oil in medium saucepan; cook leek and celery, stirring, until leek softens. Add flour and half the thyme; cook, stirring, 1 minute. Gradually stir in reserved liquid and cream; cook, stirring, until mixture boils and thickens. Stir in chicken and mustard; season to taste. Cool 10 minutes.

3 Preheat oven to 220°C/425°F. Oil eight holes in each of two 12-hole (2-tablespoon/40ml) deep flat-based patty pans.

4 Cut 16 x 7cm (2¾-inch) rounds from shortcrust pastry; press one round into each of the prepared holes. Spoon 1 tablespoon chicken mixture into each pastry case. Cut 16 x 6cm (2½-inch) rounds from puff pastry; top chicken pies with puff pastry lids. Brush lids with egg yolk; sprinkle with sesame seeds and remaining thyme. Using sharp knife, make two small slits in each lid. Bake, uncovered, about 20 minutes or until browned lightly.

prep + cook time 1½ hours
makes 16
nutritional count per pie
11.5g total fat
(5.6g saturated fat);
740kJ (177 cal);
13.5g carbohydrate;
5.1g protein; 1g fibre

tip Chicken mixture can be made the day before and kept, covered, in the refrigerator.

creamy egg and watercress sandwiches

cucumber sandwiches

1 telegraph (hothouse) cucumber (400g)

sea salt flakes

16 slices white bread (720g)

50g (1½ ounces) butter, softened

1 Peel and seed cucumber; use vegetable peeler to slice cucumber as thinly as possible. Place cucumber in a strainer or colander, sprinkle with salt. Stand 20 minutes, then rinse cucumber with cold water; drain well. Pat dry with absorbent paper.
2 Spread bread with butter. Sandwich cucumber slices between bread slices.
3 Cut crusts from bread; cut each sandwich into three fingers.

prep time 15 minutes
(+ standing) **makes** 24 fingers
nutritional count per finger
2.4g total fat
(1.2g saturated fat); 376kJ
(90 cal); 13.7g carbohydrate;
3.7g protein; 1g fibre

creamy egg and watercress sandwiches

3 eggs

¼ cup (75g) mayonnaise

1 teaspoon dijon mustard

1 tablespoon each finely chopped fresh chives and flat-leaf parsley

30g (1 ounce) butter, softened

8 slices white bread (360g)

1 cup (20g) loosely packed watercress sprigs

1 Cook eggs in small saucepan of boiling water about 7 minutes or until hard. Drain under cold water, then peel and mash eggs.
2 Combine eggs, mayonnaise, mustard and herbs in medium bowl; season to taste.

3 Spread butter over bread slices; sandwich egg mixture and watercress between bread. Cut crusts from bread; cut each sandwich into three fingers.

prep + cook time 35 minutes
makes 12 fingers
nutritional count per finger
4.9g total fat
(1.7g saturated fat);
439kJ (105 cal);
11.1g carbohydrate;
3.7g protein; 0.8g fibre

cucumber sandwiches

salmon and herb cream cheese sandwiches

salmon and herb cream cheese sandwiches

330g (2 ounces) cream cheese, softened

1 teaspoon finely chopped fresh dill

1 teaspoon finely chopped fresh chives

1 teaspoon lemon juice

1 teaspoon rinsed, drained baby capers, chopped finely

4 slices white bread (180g), crusts removed

125g (4 ounces) smoked salmon

4 large rocket leaves (arugula), trimmed

1 Combine cream cheese, dill, chives, juice and capers in small bowl. Season to taste.
2 Using rolling pin, roll over one slice of bread to flatten slightly. Spread with a quarter of the cream cheese mixture; top with a quarter of the smoked salmon and one rocket leaf, roll tightly to enclose filling.
3 Repeat with remaining bread, cream cheese mixture, smoked salmon and rocket. Trim ends then cut each roll into four slices.

prep time 20 minutes
makes 16 pieces
nutritional count per piece
1.9g total fat
(0.9g saturated fat);
213kJ (51 cal);
5.2g carbohydrate;
3.1g protein; 0.3g fibre

prawn sandwiches with lime & pepper aïoli

16 cooked medium king prawns (shrimp) (720g)

30g (1 ounce) butter, softened

8 slices white bread (360g)

1 cup (60g) shredded baby cos (romaine) lettuce

lime & pepper aïoli

½ cup (150g) mayonnaise

1 small clove garlic, crushed

½ teaspoon finely grated lime rind

2 teaspoons lime juice

¼ teaspoon cracked black pepper

1 Make lime & pepper aïoli.
2 Shell and devein prawns; halve lengthways. Stir prawns into aïoli. Season to taste.
3 Butter bread; sandwich prawn mixture and lettuce between slices. Cut crusts from bread; cut each sandwich into four triangles.

LIME & PEPPER AÏOLI Combine ingredients in medium bowl.

prep time 25 minutes
makes 16 triangles
nutritional count per triangle
5.3g total fat
(1.5g saturated fat);
518kJ (124 cal);
12g carbohydrate;
6.7g protein; 0.8g fibre

neenish tarts

1¾ cups (260g) plain (all-purpose) flour

¼ cup (40g) icing (confectioners') sugar

185g (6 ounces) cold butter, chopped coarsely

1 egg yolk

2 teaspoons iced water, approximately

⅓ cup (110g) strawberry jam (conserve)

mock cream

¾ cup (165g) caster (superfine) sugar

1½ tablespoons milk

⅓ cup (80ml) water

½ teaspoon powdered gelatine

185g (6 ounces) unsalted butter, softened

1 teaspoon vanilla extract

glace icing

1½ cups (240g) icing (confectioners') sugar

15g (½ ounce) unsalted butter, melted

2 tablespoons hot milk, approximately

pink food colouring

1 teaspoon cocoa powder

1 Process flour, icing sugar and butter until crumbly. With motor operating, add egg yolk and enough of the water to make ingredients come together. Turn dough onto floured surface, knead gently until smooth. Wrap pastry in plastic; refrigerate 30 minutes.

2 Grease two 12-hole (2-tablespoon/40ml) deep flat-based patty pans. Roll out half the pastry between sheets of baking paper until 3mm (⅛ inch) thick. Cut out 12 x 7.5cm (3-inch) rounds; press rounds into holes of one pan. Prick bases of cases well with a fork. Repeat with remaining pastry. Refrigerate 30 minutes.

3 Preheat oven to 220°C/425°F.

4 Bake cases about 12 minutes. Stand cases 5 minutes before transferring to wire rack to cool.

5 Meanwhile, make mock cream and glacé icing.

6 Divide jam between pastry cases; fill cases with mock cream, level tops with spatula. Spread pink icing over half of each tart; cover remaining half with the chocolate icing.

MOCK CREAM Stir sugar, milk and ¼ cup of the water in small saucepan over low heat, without boiling, until sugar dissolves. Sprinkle gelatine over remaining water in small jug, stand 5 minutes then stir into milk mixture until gelatine dissolves. Cool to room temperature. Beat butter and extract in small bowl with electric mixer until as white as possible. With motor operating, gradually beat in cold milk mixture; beat until light and fluffy.

GLACÉ ICING Sift icing sugar into medium bowl; stir in butter and enough of the milk to make a thick paste. Divide icing between two small heatproof bowls; tint icing in one bowl with pink colouring. Stir sifted cocoa into other bowl of icing until combined. Stir each bowl over small saucepan of simmering water until icing is spreadable.

prep + cook time 1¾ hours (+ refrigeration & cooling)
makes 24
nutritional count per tart
13.6g total fat
(8.8g saturated fat);
1016kJ (243 cal);
29.7g carbohydrate;
1.6g protein; 0.5g fibre

rosewater meringue kisses

2 egg whites

½ cup (110g) caster (superfine) sugar

1 teaspoon rosewater

pink food colouring

2 tablespoons pouring cream

90g (3 ounces) white eating chocolate, chopped finely

4 fresh or thawed frozen raspberries

1 Preheat oven to 120°C/250°F. Grease oven trays; line with baking paper.
2 Beat egg whites, sugar, rosewater and a few drops of pink food colouring in small bowl with electric mixer about 10 minutes or until sugar is dissolved and mixture is thick and glossy.
3 Spoon mixture into piping bag fitted with 2cm (¾-inch) fluted tube; pipe 4cm (1½-inch) stars, about 2cm (¾-inch), apart onto oven trays. Bake meringues about 50 minutes or until dry to touch. Cool on trays.
4 Meanwhile, bring cream to the boil in small saucepan. Remove from heat; add chocolate, stir until smooth.
5 Push raspberries through a fine sieve over a bowl to make raspberry purée – you will need 2 teaspoons. Stir raspberry puree into chocolate with a few drops of pink food colouring. Refrigerate for 20 minutes or until the filling is spreadable.
6 Sandwich meringues with raspberry chocolate filling.

prep + cook time 1¼ hours (+ cooling & refrigeration)
makes 20
nutritional count per kiss
2.4g total fat
(1.5g saturated fat);
228kJ (54 cal);
8g carbohydrate;
0.7g protein; 0g fibre

mulberry powder puffs

2 eggs

⅓ cup (75g) caster (superfine) sugar

2 tablespoons plain (all-purpose) flour

2 tablespoons self-raising flour

2 tablespoons cornflour (cornstarch)

½ cup (125ml) thickened (heavy) cream

2 tablespoons icing (confectioners') sugar

½ cup (70g) finely chopped fresh mulberries

1 Preheat oven to 180°C/350°F. Butter and flour two 12-hole (1-tablespoon/20ml) shallow round-based patty pans.
2 Beat eggs and caster sugar in small bowl with electric mixer about 5 minutes or until thick and creamy. Sift combined flours and cornflour twice onto baking paper, then sift over egg mixture; fold flour into egg mixture.
3 Drop level tablespoons of mixture into pan holes. Bake about 12 minutes; immediately turn puffs onto wire racks to cool.
4 To make mulberry cream: Beat cream and half the icing sugar in small bowl with electric mixer until soft peaks form; fold in berries.
5 Sandwich puffs with mulberry cream just before serving. Dust with sifted remaining icing sugar.

prep + cook time 1 hour (+ cooling) **makes** 12
nutritional count per puff
4.8g total fat (2.8g saturated fat); 403kJ (96 cal); 18.6g carbohydrate; 1.6g protein; 0.3g fibre

tips Use any fresh berries you like in this recipe. If you only have one patty pan, bake the first batch, then wash, butter and flour the pan again before baking the next lot.

raspberry cream sponge

4 eggs

¾ cup (165g) caster (superfine) sugar

⅔ cup (100g) wheaten cornflour (cornstarch)

¼ cup (30g) custard powder (instant pudding mix)

1 teaspoon cream of tartar

½ teaspoon bicarbonate of soda (baking soda)

¾ cup (240g) raspberry jam (conserve)

1½ cups (375ml) thickened (heavy) cream, whipped

raspberry glacé icing

45g (1½ ounces) fresh raspberries

2 cups (320g) icing (confectioners') sugar

15g (½ ounce) butter, softened

2 teaspoons hot water, approximately

1 Preheat oven to 180°C/350°F. Grease deep 22cm (9-inch) square cake pan with butter.
2 Beat eggs and sugar in small bowl with electric mixer about 10 minutes or until thick and creamy and sugar has dissolved; transfer to large bowl.
3 Sift dry ingredients twice onto baking paper, then sift over egg mixture; fold dry ingredients into egg mixture. Spread mixture into pan.
4 Bake sponge about 25 minutes. Turn sponge immediately onto baking-paper-covered wire rack, then turn top-side up to cool.
5 Make raspberry glacé icing.
6 Split sponge in half. Sandwich with jam and cream. Spread sponge with raspberry icing; top with extra fresh berries, if you like.

RASPBERRY GLACÉ ICING Push the raspberries through a fine sieve into small heatproof bowl; discard solids. Sift icing sugar into same bowl; stir in butter and enough of the water to make a thick paste. Place bowl over small saucepan of simmering water; stir until icing is spreadable.

prep + cook time 50 minutes (+ cooling) **serves** 16
nutritional count per serving 10.8g total fat (6.6g saturated fat); 1053kJ (252 cal); 37.6g carbohydrate; 2.3g protein; 0.4g fibre

Teacakes are best eaten warm from the oven. To make a light and fluffy teacake, it is important to cream the butter, extract, sugar and egg thoroughly until the mixture is as light and white as possible.

cinnamon teacake

60g (2 ounces) butter, softened

1 teaspoon vanilla extract

⅔ cup caster (superfine) sugar

1 egg

1 cup (150g) self-raising flour

⅓ cup (80ml) milk

10g (½ ounce) butter, extra

1 teaspoon ground cinnamon

1 tablespoon caster (superfine) sugar, extra

1 Preheat oven to 180°C/350°F. Grease deep 20cm (8-inch) round cake pan; line base with baking paper.
2 Beat butter, extract, sugar and egg in small bowl with electric mixer until light and fluffy.
3 Stir in sifted flour, and the milk; stir gently until smooth.
4 Spread mixture into pan; bake about 30 minutes. Turn, top-side up, onto wire rack.
5 Meanwhile, melt extra butter; brush over top of hot cake, then sprinkle with combined cinnamon and extra sugar while hot.

prep + cook time 50 minutes
serves 8
nutritional count per serving
8.4g total fat
(5.2g saturated fat);
936kJ (224 cal);
34.6g carbohydrate;
3.1g protein; 0.7g fibre

tip Recipe is best made on the day of serving.

serving suggestion Serve warm with butter.

cocktails & canapes

haloumi and asparagus bites with lemony dressing

340g (11 ounces) asparagus, trimmed

250g (8 ounces) haloumi cheese

lemony dressing

1 tablespoon rinsed, drained baby capers, chopped finely

1 tablespoon olive oil

2 teaspoons finely grated lemon rind

1 tablespoon lemon juice

½ teaspoon white (granulated) sugar

1 Make lemony dressing.
2 Cut asparagus into 3cm (1¼-inch) lengths. Boil, steam or microwave until barely tender; rinse under cold water, drain.
3 Cut haloumi into 1cm (½-inch) slices, then into 1cm x 3cm (½-inch x 1¼-inch) pieces. Thread one piece of asparagus, one piece of haloumi, then another piece of asparagus close together onto each toothpick.
4 Cook bites in large oiled frying pan over high heat about 30 seconds each side or until browned lightly.
5 Serve bites immediately, drizzled with dressing.

LEMONY DRESSING Place ingredients in a screw-top jar; shake well.

prep + cook time 55 minutes
makes 40 pieces
nutritional count per piece
1.5g total fat
(0.8g saturated fat);
83kJ (20 cal);
1.5g carbohydrate;
0.3g protein; 0.2g fibre

tip Use strong wooden toothpicks for this recipe or short pieces of bamboo skewers.

martini

Place 1 small rinsed seeded green olive and a dash of dry vermouth into chilled ⅔-cup cocktail glass; swirl vermouth in glass to coat. Place 1 cup ice cubes and 45ml (1½-fluid ounces) gin in cocktail shaker; shake vigorously. Strain into glass.

prep time 5 minutes **serves** 1
nutritional count per serving 0.3g total fat (0g saturated fat); 512kJ (122 cal); 5.4g carbohydrate; 0.2g protein; 0.3g fibre

vodka martini

Place 1 small rinsed seeded green olive and a dash of dry vermouth into chilled ⅔-cup cocktail glass; swirl vermouth in glass to coat. Place 1 cup ice cubes and 45ml (1½-fluid ounces) vodka in cocktail shaker; shake vigorously. Strain into glass.

prep time 5 minutes **serves** 1
nutritional count per serving 0.3g total fat (0g saturated fat); 512kJ (122 cal); 5.4g carbohydrate; 0.2g protein; 0.3g fibre

manhattan

Place 1 maraschino cherry into chilled ½-cup cocktail glass; rub the cut edge of an orange over the rim of the glass. Place ½ cup ice cubes, 45ml (1½-fluid ounces) whiskey, 15ml (½-fluid ounce) sweet vermouth and dash of Angostura Bitters in a mixing glass; stir gently. Strain into glass.

prep time 5 minutes **serves** 1
nutritional count per serving 0g total fat
(0g saturated fat); 526kJ (126 cal);
3.2g carbohydrate; 0g protein; 0g fibre

tom collins

Place 60ml (2-fluid ounces) gin, 80ml (2½-fluid ounces) lemon juice, 2 teaspoons pure icing sugar (confectioners' sugar) and 80ml (2½-fluid ounces) soda water into chilled ice-filled 1½-cup highball glass; stir gently. Garnish with maraschino cherry and curls of lemon peel.

prep time 5 minutes **serves** 1
nutritional count per serving 0.2g total fat
(0g saturated fat); 530kJ (127 cal);
10.7g carbohydrate; 0.6g protein; 0.1g fibre

devilled eggs

12 eggs

1 tablespoon dijon mustard

⅔ cup (200g) mayonnaise

2 tablespoons each finely chopped fresh chives and flat-leaf parsley

1 Cook eggs in large saucepan of boiling water about 7 minutes or until hard. Drain under cold water, then peel and halve each egg.
2 Carefully scoop egg yolks from whites into medium bowl. Place egg whites on serving platter.
3 Mash egg yolks with mustard and mayonnaise until smooth; stir in herbs, season to taste.
4 Spoon egg yolk mixture into piping bag fitted with 1.5cm (¾-inch) fluted tube; pipe mixture into egg white halves. Serve eggs sprinkled with extra parsley or chives, if you like.

prep + cook time 45 minutes
makes 24
nutritional count per egg
5.3g total fat
(1.1g saturated fat);
284kJ (68 cal);
1.7g carbohydrate;
3.4g protein; 0.1g fibre

oozy cheese fritters

60g (2 ounces) butter

1 teaspoon mustard powder

½ teaspoon sweet paprika

½ teaspoon chilli powder

⅓ cup (50g) plain (all-purpose) flour

1½ cups (375ml) milk

¾ cup (90g) coarsely grated gouda cheese

1 cup (100g) coarsely grated mozzarella cheese

4 green onions (scallions), chopped finely

¼ cup (35g) plain (all-purpose) flour, extra

¾ cup (75g) packaged breadcrumbs

2 eggs

vegetable oil, for deep-frying

mint salsa

1 cup loosely packed fresh flat-leaf parsley leaves

½ cup loosely packed fresh mint leaves

3 teaspoons red wine vinegar

½ teaspoon white (granulated) sugar

2 teaspoons rinsed, drained baby capers

2 tablespoons olive oil

1 Melt butter in medium saucepan, stir in spices and flour; cook, stirring, over medium heat until mixture bubbles. Remove from heat, gradually stir in milk; stir over heat until mixture boils and thickens. Remove from heat, stir in cheeses until smooth; stir in onion, season to taste. Cover sauce, refrigerate about 3 hours or until firm.
2 Make mint salsa.
3 Place extra flour and breadcrumbs in separate medium shallow bowls. Beat eggs lightly in another medium shallow bowl. Drop rounded teaspoonfuls of cheese sauce into flour, coat lightly; shake off excess. Dip in egg, then in breadcrumbs; place on tray. Cover; refrigerate 30 minutes.
4 Heat oil in wok or deep, wide saucepan to 180°C/350°F. Deep-fry fritters, in batches, until golden brown; drain on absorbent paper. Serve fritters with salsa.

MINT SALSA Blend or process ingredients until smooth.

prep + cook time 50 minutes (+ refrigeration) **makes** 72
nutritional count per fritter
2.9g total fat
(1.2g saturated fat);
159kJ (38 cal);
1.9g carbohydrate;
1.3g protein; 0.2g fibre

tip Make sure the oil for deep frying is very hot, only deep-fry the fritters for a few seconds, or they will break open.

sticky chicken with pickled cucumber

300g (9½ ounces) chicken thigh fillets, chopped coarsely

1 tablespoon kecap manis

1cm (½-inch) piece fresh ginger (5g), grated

2½ teaspoons white (granulated) sugar

¼ cup (60ml) rice vinegar

½ teaspoon salt

4 lebanese cucumbers (520g)

1 fresh long red chilli, chopped finely

1 Combine chicken, kecap manis, ginger and ½ teaspoon of the sugar in large bowl. Cover; refrigerate 30 minutes.
2 Stir vinegar, salt and remaining sugar in medium bowl until sugar dissolves. Cut cucumbers into 1cm (½-inch) slices; using teaspoon or melon baller, remove and discard about half the seeds from each slice. Add cucumber to vinegar mixture, stand 10 minutes; drain on absorbent paper.
3 Cook chicken in heated oiled large frying pan until cooked through.
4 Top each cucumber slice with a piece of chicken; sprinkle with a little chilli.

prep + cook time 40 minutes (+ refrigeration) **makes** 30
nutritional count per piece
0.7g total fat
(0.2g saturated fat);
75kJ (18 cal);
0.8g carbohydrate;
2g protein; 0.2g fibre

tip Be careful not to push the melon baller or teaspoon right through the cucumber, as it must remain intact to hold the filling; just make a small indent in the flesh.

asparagus, tomato and goat's cheese tarts

170g (5½ ounces) asparagus

125g (4 ounces) cherry tomatoes

1 teaspoon finely grated lemon rind

1 tablespoon olive oil

¼ cup loosely packed fresh basil leaves, shredded finely

20 shortcrust pastry cases

70g (2½ ounces) marinated goat's cheese, drained

1 Trim asparagus; slice thinly. Boil, steam or microwave asparagus until tender; drain. Rinse under cold water; drain.

2 Halve tomatoes; cut into thin wedges.

3 Combine asparagus and tomato in medium bowl with rind, oil and half the basil; season to taste.

4 Divide half the asparagus and tomato mixture into pastry cases; top with cheese, then remaining asparagus and tomato mixture. Sprinkle with remaining basil.

prep + cook time 25 minutes
makes 20
nutritional count per tart
7.5g total fat
(3.8g saturated fat);
485kJ (116 cal);
9.9g carbohydrate;
2.2g protein; 0.6g fibre

tip You can use fetta cheese in place of the goat's cheese.

scallops with pea puree

2 medium tomatoes (300g), peeled, seeded, chopped finely

1 tablespoon olive oil

1 tablespoon verjuice

2 tablespoons fresh chervil leaves

2 teaspoons finely grated lemon rind

24 scallops on the half shell, roe removed

pea puree

1½ cups (180g) frozen peas

¼ cup (60ml) pouring cream

2 tablespoons hot water, approximately

1 Make pea puree.
2 Combine tomato, oil, verjuice, chervil and rind in medium bowl.
3 Remove scallops from shells; wash and dry shells. Spoon pea puree into shells.
4 Heat oiled large frying pan; cook scallops about 30 seconds each side or until browned lightly but still soft in the centre.
5 Place scallops on pea puree; top scallops with tomato mixture.

PEA PUREE Boil, steam or microwave peas until tender; drain. Blend peas with cream and enough of the water to give a thick pouring consistency; season to taste.

prep + cook time 30 minutes
makes 24
nutritional count per piece
2.1g total fat
(0.9g saturated fat);
167kJ (40 cal);
1.1g carbohydrate;
4g protein; 0.5g fibre

lamb rogan josh with rösti

2 teaspoons vegetable oil

1 medium brown onion (150g), chopped finely

1 clove garlic, crushed

1cm (½-inch) piece fresh ginger (5g), grated

600g (1¼ pounds) lamb fillets, chopped finely

2 tablespoons rogan josh curry paste

2 medium tomatoes (300g), seeded, chopped finely

2 tablespoons lemon juice

2 tablespoons finely chopped fresh coriander (cilantro)

rösti

2 medium potatoes (400g), unpeeled

40g (1½ ounces) butter, melted

1 Make rösti.
2 Meanwhile, heat half the oil in large frying pan; cook onion, garlic and ginger, stirring, until onion softens. Remove from pan.
3 Heat remaining oil in pan; cook lamb until browned. Return onion mixture to pan with paste; cook, stirring, until fragrant. Remove pan from heat. Stir in tomato, juice and coriander; season to taste.
4 Divide lamb mixture into rösti cases; serve immediately.

RÖSTI Place unpeeled potatoes in medium saucepan, cover with cold water, cover pan; bring to the boil. Boil about 20 minutes or until potatoes are almost tender; drain, cool and peel. Coarsely grate potatoes into medium bowl; stir in butter. Preheat oven to 250°C/480°F. Press 1 teaspoon potato mixture over base and half-way up side of each hole in two 24-hole (1-tablespoon/20ml) mini muffin pans. Bake rösti about 10 minutes or until browned around the edges. Remove rösti from oven; stand 30 seconds, then remove from pans. Drain on absorbent paper.

prep + cook time 1 hour
makes 48
nutritional count per rösti
1.6g total fat
(0.7g saturated fat);
134kJ (32 cal);
1.2g carbohydrate;
3g protein; 0.3g fibre

tips We used desiree potatoes, (a thin-skinned red potato) for the rösti. There is no need to oil the muffin pans unless they are scratched.

dinner party

prawn cocktail

1kg (2 pounds) cooked medium king prawns (shrimp)

⅓ cup (100g) mayonnaise

2 tablespoons pouring cream

1 tablespoon tomato sauce (ketchup)

1 teaspoon worcestershire sauce

½ teaspoon Tabasco sauce

½ teaspoon dijon mustard

2 teaspoons lemon juice

8 baby cos (romaine) lettuce leaves

1 lemon (140g), cut into wedges

1 Shell and devein prawns.
2 Combine mayonnaise, cream, sauces, mustard and juice in small bowl; season to taste.
3 Divide lettuce between four glasses; top with prawns, drizzle with sauce.

prep time 30 minutes **serves** 4
nutritional count per serving
13.2g total fat (3.9g saturated fat); 1070kJ (256 cal); 7.3g carbohydrate; 26.6g protein; 1g fibre

scotch eggs

7 eggs

1 tablespoon plain (all-purpose) flour

1 tablespoon milk

500g (1 pound) sausage mince

⅔ cup (70g) packaged breadcrumbs

vegetable oil, for deep-frying

herb mayonnaise

½ cup (150g) mayonnaise

1 tablespoon lemon juice

1 tablespoon each finely chopped fresh chives and oregano

1 Cook six of the eggs in medium saucepan of boiling water about 7 minutes or until hard. Drain under cold water. When cool enough to handle, peel eggs.
2 Make herb mayonnaise.
3 Place flour in small shallow bowl. Beat remaining egg and milk in small bowl until combined. Toss hard-boiled eggs in flour; shake off excess. Divide sausage mince into six portions; using floured hands, shape mince around each egg. Dip in egg mixture, then in breadcrumbs.
4 Heat oil in a deep, wide saucepan to 180°C/350°F. Deep-fry eggs, in batches, until mince is browned and cooked through. Drain on absorbent paper. Serve with herb mayonnaise.

HERB MAYONNAISE Combine ingredients in small bowl; season to taste.

prep + cook time 55 minutes
makes 6
nutritional count per egg
42.6g total fat
(12.6g saturated fat);
2211kJ (529 cal);
16.6g carbohydrate;
19.7g protein; 2.2g fibre

goat's cheese gateau

½ cup (140g) bottled roasted red capsicum (bell pepper), drained

250g (8 ounces) cream cheese, softened

2 tablespoons lemon juice

360g (11½ ounces) goat's cheese, softened

¼ cup (60ml) pouring cream

1 tablespoon finely chopped preserved lemon rind

2 teaspoons finely grated lemon rind

2 tablespoons finely chopped fresh chervil

grape juice glaze

¾ cup (180ml) grape juice

2 teaspoons powdered gelatine

1 tablespoon caster (superfine) sugar

¼ cup (60ml) port

1 Grease 20cm (8-inch) (closed) springform pan; line base and side with baking paper.

2 Blend or process capsicum, cream cheese and half the juice until combined; season to taste. Spread into pan. Cover mixture; refrigerate 30 minutes.

3 Blend or process goat's cheese, cream, preserved lemon, lemon rind, chervil and remaining juice until combined; season to taste. Spread evenly over capsicum mixture. Cover; refrigerate 30 minutes.

4 Meanwhile, make grape juice glaze; cool.

5 Pour glaze over cheese mixture. Cover; refrigerate overnight.

6 Remove gateau from pan. Serve cold with bagel crisps and salad leaves, if you like.

GRAPE JUICE GLAZE Place ¼ cup of the grape juice and the gelatine in a small heatproof jug; stand 5 minutes, then stand jug in pan of simmering water, stir until gelatine is dissolved, cool. Stir remaining grape juice and sugar in small saucepan over low heat until sugar dissolves; cool, then stir in the port and the gelatine mixture.

prep + cook time 1 hour (+ refrigeration & cooling)
serves 16
nutritional count per serving
10.4g total fat
(6.7g saturated fat);
556kJ (133 cal);
4.4g carbohydrate;
4.9g protein; 0.2g fibre

tip Preserved lemons can be bought from delis and some supermarkets. Remove a piece of lemon from the jar, discard the lemon flesh. Rinse the rind under water; dry, then chop finely.

melon in prosciutto

chicken terrine

14 slices prosciutto (210g)

600g (1¼ pounds) chicken thigh fillets

600g (1¼ pounds) chicken breast fillets

¼ cup (35g) unsalted pistachios, chopped coarsely

3 teaspoons dijon mustard

1 teaspoon finely grated lemon rind

¼ cup coarsely chopped fresh flat-leaf parsley

1 Preheat oven to 200°C/400°F. Oil 8cm x 20cm (3¼-inch x 8-inch) loaf pan; line base and two long sides with baking paper, extending paper 5cm (2 inches) over sides.
2 Line base and sides of pan with prosciutto, slightly overlapping the slices and allowing overhang on long sides of pan.
3 Chop all the chicken into 2cm (¾-inch) pieces. Process half the chicken until minced finely. Combine chicken mince, chopped chicken and remaining ingredients in large bowl; season. Press into pan. Fold prosciutto and baking paper over to cover; cover tightly with foil.
4 Place pan in medium baking dish; pour in enough boiling water to come halfway up side of pan. Bake terrine 1 hour. Drain juices from pan. Cool; weight with another dish filled with heavy cans. Refrigerate 3 hours.
5 Turn terrine onto plate; slice thickly to serve.

prep + cook time 1½ hours (+ refrigeration) **serves** 8
nutritional count per serving
13.3g total fat
(3.7g saturated fat);
1116kJ (267 cal);
0.8g carbohydrate;
35.7g protein; 0.5g fibre

melon in prosciutto

1 small rockmelon (1.3kg), halved lengthways

12 slices prosciutto (180g)

2 tablespoons olive oil

¼ cup loosely packed fresh flat-leaf parsley leaves

1 Peel and seed rockmelon; cut into 12 wedges.
2 Wrap prosciutto around melon wedges.
3 Serve melon drizzled with oil and sprinkled with parsley.

prep time 15 minutes **serves** 4
nutritional count per serving
11.9g total fat
(2.2g saturated fat);
802kJ (192 cal);
10.9g carbohydrate;
9.4g protein; 2.5g fibre

tip Use good-quality extra virgin olive oil for the best flavour.

chicken terrine

beef wellington

800g (1½-pound) piece beef fillet

1 tablespoon olive oil

25g (¾ ounce) butter

1 small brown onion (80g), chopped finely

125g (4 ounces) button mushrooms, chopped finely

150g (4½ ounces) chicken or duck liver pâté

2 sheets puff pastry

1 egg, beaten lightly

1 Tie beef securely with kitchen string. Heat oil in large frying pan; cook beef until browned all over. Wrap beef in foil; cool.
2 Heat butter in same pan; cook onion and mushrooms, stirring, until tender. Cool.
3 Preheat oven to 240°C/425°F. Line oven tray with baking paper.
4 Stir pâté in medium bowl until soft. Remove string from beef. Spread pâté all over beef; season.
5 Roll out both pastry sheets, slightly overlapping to make one large sheet, on lightly floured surface into a rectangle large enough to enclose the beef; moisten edges with water.
6 Place mushroom mixture down centre of pastry; place beef on top of mixture. Fold pastry over beef to enclose; trim excess pastry and press edges to seal. Place beef, seam-side down, on tray; brush with egg then cut small slits in top of pastry.
7 Bake beef 10 minutes. Reduce oven temperature to 200°C/400°F; bake a further 20 minutes or until browned lightly. Slice beef thickly to serve.

prep + cook time 1½ hours (+ cooling) **serves** 4
nutritional count per serving 52.2g total fat (23g saturated fat); 3449kJ (825 cal); 31.9g carbohydrate; 56.4g protein; 2.7g fibre

tips It is important to trim off any excess pastry when covering the beef. Don't have the pastry too thick at the joins or the pastry will not cook through. To decorate, cut small leaves from pastry scraps and secure them to the beef wellington with a little of the egg before baking.

serving suggestion Serve with steamed vegetables.

steak diane

1 tablespoon olive oil

4 x 150g (4½-ounce) beef fillet steaks

⅓ cup (80ml) brandy

2 cloves garlic, crushed

¼ cup (60ml) worcestershire sauce

1 cup (250ml) pouring cream

1 tablespoon finely chopped fresh flat-leaf parsley

1 Heat oil in large frying pan; cook steaks until cooked as desired. Remove from pan; cover to keep warm.

2 Add brandy to pan; bring to the boil. Add garlic, sauce and cream; cook, stirring, 3 minutes or until sauce thickens slightly.

3 Remove pan from heat; stir in parsley, season to taste.

4 Serve steaks with sauce.

prep + cook time 25 minutes
serves 4
nutritional count per serving
40.6g total fat
(22.3g saturated fat);
2324kJ (556 cal);
5.2g carbohydrate;
33.2g protein; 0.4g fibre

serving suggestion Serve with shoestring chips and a leafy green salad.

duck a l'orange

2kg (4-pound) whole duck

30g (1 ounce) butter, melted

1 large orange (300g)

1 tablespoon caster (superfine) sugar

1 tablespoon white vinegar

2 teaspoons lemon juice

2 cups (500ml) chicken stock

2 teaspoons arrowroot

1 tablespoon water

½ cup (125ml) orange-flavoured liqueur

1 Preheat oven to 180°C/350°F.
2 Rinse duck under cold water; pat dry inside and out with absorbent paper. Tie legs together with kitchen string; tuck wings under duck. Place duck in oiled large baking dish; brush butter all over duck, season. Roast, uncovered, about 1 hour, basting occasionally.
3 Meanwhile, peel orange thinly. Discard any white pith from peel; cut peel into thin strips. Juice orange (you need ½ cup juice).
4 Combine rind, orange juice, sugar, vinegar, lemon juice and stock in medium saucepan; bring to the boil. Boil, uncovered, without stirring, until liquid is reduced by half. Gradually stir in blended arrowroot and the water; cook, stirring, until sauce almost boils and thickens. Remove from heat; stir in liqueur.
5 Remove baking dish from oven; drain pan juices from dish. Pour orange sauce over duck; roast, uncovered, a further 30 minutes, basting with sauce occasionally, until duck is tender and well-glazed.
6 Serve duck with orange sauce.

prep + cook time 2 hours
serves 4
nutritional count per serving
22.5g total fat
(9.2g saturated fat);
2420kJ (579 cal);
23.3g carbohydrate;
57.5g protein; 0.2g fibre

serving suggestion Serve with steamed green beans, potatoes and carrots.

guard of honour

½ cup each firmly packed fresh flat-leaf parsley and mint leaves

¼ cup loosely packed fresh oregano leaves

4 cloves garlic, chopped coarsely

⅓ cup (80ml) olive oil

2 x 8 french-trimmed lamb cutlet racks (720g)

1kg (2 pounds) baby new potatoes

1 Preheat oven to 200°C/400°F.

2 Blend or process herbs, garlic and half the oil until smooth; season to taste.

3 Place lamb racks in large oiled baking dish, leaning against one another, interlacing cutlet bones so racks stand upright. Press herb mixture onto each rack.

4 Meanwhile, boil, steam or microwave potatoes until just tender; drain. Cut potatoes in half, place on oiled oven tray; drizzle with remaining oil, season.

5 Roast lamb and potatoes, uncovered, about 35 minutes or until lamb is cooked as desired. Remove lamb from oven, cover; stand 10 minutes. Roast potatoes a further 10 minutes or until browned lightly.

6 Serve lamb with roasted potatoes, and steamed or roasted vegetables of your choice.

prep + cook time 1 hour
serves 4
nutritional count per serving
26.9g total fat
(6.6g saturated fat);
2086kJ (499 cal);
33.6g carbohydrate;
26.7g protein; 6.3g fibre

tips You can use skewers or toothpicks to help keep the guard of honour secure.
Wrap the ends of cutlet bones with small pieces of foil to stop them burning during roasting. To make paper booties for the roast: Cut 10cm (4 inch) squares from paper (printer paper is fine). Fold squares in half gently without creasing at the fold. Make cuts 3mm (⅛-inch) apart through the fold to within 5mm (¼ inch) of the cut edges. Attach to bones by wrapping straight ends of paper strips around bones; secure with tape. This gives a single frill. For multiple frills, place a number of frilled squares in layers on top of each other and tape together.

shepherd's pie

30g (1 ounce) butter

1 medium brown onion (150g), chopped finely

1 medium carrot (120g), chopped finely

½ teaspoon dried mixed herbs

4 cups (750g) finely chopped cooked lamb

¼ cup (70g) tomato paste

¼ cup (60ml) tomato sauce (ketchup)

2 tablespoons worcestershire sauce

2 cups (500ml) beef stock

2 tablespoons plain (all-purpose) flour

⅓ cup (80ml) water

potato topping

5 medium potatoes (1kg), chopped coarsely

60g (2 ounces) butter, chopped coarsely

¼ cup (60ml) milk

1 Preheat oven to 200°C/400°F. Oil deep 2.5-litre (10-cup) ovenproof dish.

2 Make potato topping.

3 Heat butter in large saucepan; cook onion and carrot, stirring, until vegetables are tender. Add mixed herbs and lamb; cook, stirring, 2 minutes. Stir in paste, sauces and stock, then blended flour and the water; cook, stirring, until mixture boils and thickens. Season to taste. Pour mixture into dish.

4 Spoon potato topping into piping bag fitted with a large fluted nozzle; pipe topping over lamb mixture.

5 Bake pie 20 minutes or until browned lightly.

POTATO TOPPING Boil, steam or microwave potato until tender; drain. Mash potato in medium bowl with butter and milk until smooth; season to taste.

prep + cook time 1 hour
serves 4
nutritional count per serving
36.2g total fat (20.2g saturated fat); 2976kJ (712 cal); 44.7g carbohydrate; 48.8g protein; 6.6g fibre

corned beef with parsley sauce

1.5kg (3-pound) piece beef corned silverside

2 dried bay leaves

6 black peppercorns

1 large brown onion (200g), quartered

1 large carrot (180g), chopped coarsely

1 tablespoon brown malt vinegar

¼ cup (50g) firmly packed light brown sugar

parsley sauce

30g (1 ounce) butter

¼ cup (35g) plain (all-purpose) flour

2½ cups (625ml) milk

⅓ cup (40g) coarsely grated cheddar cheese

⅓ cup finely chopped fresh flat-leaf parsley

1 tablespoon mild mustard

1 Place beef, bay leaves, peppercorns, onion, carrot, vinegar and half the sugar in large saucepan. Add enough water to just cover beef; simmer, covered, about 2 hours or until beef is tender. Cool beef 1 hour in liquid in pan.

2 Remove beef from pan; discard liquid. Sprinkle sheet of foil with remaining sugar, wrap beef in foil; stand 20 minutes then slice thinly.

3 Meanwhile, make parsley sauce. Serve sliced corned beef with parsley sauce.

PARSLEY SAUCE Heat butter in small saucepan, add flour; cook, stirring, until mixture thickens and bubbles. Gradually stir in milk; cook, stirring, until sauce boils and thickens. Remove from heat; stir in cheese, parsley and mustard. Season to taste.

prep + cook time 2¼ hours (+ cooling & standing) **serves** 4
nutritional count per serving 35.8g total fat (19.3g saturated fat); 3520kJ (842 cal); 31g carbohydrate; 97g protein; 2.5g fibre

serving suggestion Serve with roasted potatoes and steamed green beans.

roast balsamic chicken with garlic bread sauce

1.8kg (3½-pound) whole chicken

⅓ cup (80ml) balsamic vinegar

1 tablespoon dijon mustard

1 tablespoon olive oil

2 sprigs fresh rosemary

500g (1 pound) cherry truss tomatoes

2 sprigs fresh thyme

garlic bread sauce

4 cloves garlic, bruised

2 fresh bay leaves

1¾ cups (430ml) milk

1½ cups (110g) stale breadcrumbs

30g (1 ounce) butter

½ cup (125ml) pouring cream

1 Rinse chicken under cold water. Pat dry inside and out with absorbent paper. Combine vinegar, mustard and oil in large bowl, add chicken; turn to coat chicken in marinade. Cover; refrigerate 3 hours.

2 Preheat oven to 200°C/400°F.

3 Place chicken in large baking dish; reserve marinade. Place one rosemary sprig into chicken cavity. Tie legs together with kitchen string; season. Roast, uncovered, about 1½ hours or until cooked through, basting with reserved marinade. Add tomatoes to the dish for the last 10 minutes of cooking time.

4 Meanwhile, make garlic bread sauce.

5 Tuck thyme and remaining rosemary between drumsticks; serve chicken with sauce and tomatoes.

GARLIC BREAD SAUCE Bring garlic, bay leaves and milk to the boil in small saucepan. Remove from heat, stand 30 minutes. Strain milk mixture, discard solids; return milk mixture to same pan. Stir in breadcrumbs and butter; cook, stirring, over low heat, about 10 minutes or until thick. Add cream, stir until heated through; season to taste.

prep + cook time 2 hours (+ refrigeration & standing)

serves 6

nutritional count per serving
47g total fat
(19g saturated fat);
2717kJ (650 cal);
19.9g carbohydrate;
36.3g protein; 2.6g fibre

turkey and cranberry meatloaf

10 slices prosciutto (150g)

1 medium brown onion (150g), grated coarsely

2 green onions (scallions), sliced thinly

2 cloves garlic, crushed

750g (1½ pounds) minced (ground) turkey

2 tablespoons tomato sauce (ketchup)

1 tablespoon worcestershire sauce

1 egg yolk

½ cup (35g) stale breadcrumbs

⅓ cup finely chopped fresh flat-leaf parsley

½ cup (160g) cranberry sauce

2 tablespoons orange juice

1 Preheat oven to 200°C/400°F.
2 Oil 15cm x 20cm (6-inch x 8-inch) loaf pan. Line base and sides of pan with prosciutto, slightly overlapping the slices and allowing overhang on long sides of pan.
3 Combine both onions, garlic, turkey mince, sauces, egg yolk, breadcrumbs and parsley in large bowl; season. Press into pan. Fold prosciutto over to cover turkey mixture. Place pan on oven tray. Bake 45 minutes.
4 Meanwhile, combine cranberry sauce and juice in small bowl.
5 Remove meatloaf from oven; drain juices from pan. Carefully invert meatloaf onto wire rack. Place rack over oven tray. Brush meatloaf with cranberry mixture; return to oven, bake about 15 minutes or until browned and cooked through.

prep + cook time 1½ hours
serves 4
nutritional count per serving
12.2g total fat
(3.4g saturated fat);
1760kJ (421 cal);
28.8g carbohydrate;
47.7g protein; 1.7g fibre

note Cranberry sauce is made from cranberries cooked in sugar syrup; it has an astringent flavour that goes well with poultry and meats.

pork loin with apple sauce

2.5kg (5-pound) boneless loin of pork, rind on

2 sprigs fresh rosemary

1 tablespoon olive oil

1 tablespoon coarse cooking salt

3 large apples (600g), peeled, cored, sliced thickly

¼ cup (60ml) water

1 teaspoon white (granulated) sugar

pinch ground cinnamon

1 Preheat oven to 240°C/475°F.

2 Tie pork at 2cm (¾-inch) intervals with kitchen string; tuck rosemary under string. Place pork in large baking dish; rub with oil then salt.

3 Roast pork, uncovered, about 40 minutes or until skin blisters. Drain excess fat from dish.

4 Reduce oven temperature to 180°C/350°F; roast pork a further 1 hour. Cover pork loosely with foil; stand 15 minutes.

5 Meanwhile, place apple and the water in medium saucepan; simmer, covered, 5 minutes. Uncover; simmer about 5 minutes or until apple is soft. Remove from heat; stir in sugar and cinnamon.

6 Serve pork with apple sauce.

prep + cook time 2 hours (+ standing) **serves** 8
nutritional count per serving 72g total fat (24.1g saturated fat); 3762kJ (900 cal); 7.7g carbohydrate; 56.7g protein; 1.1g fibre

tip Just loosely cover the pork when standing; if you cover it tightly, the crackling will lose all its crunchy deliciousness and turn soft.

serving suggestion Serve with roasted vegetables.

desserts

classic trifle

85g (3 ounces) raspberry jelly crystals

250g (8-ounce) sponge cake, cut into 2.5cm (1-inch) pieces

¼ cup (60ml) sweet sherry

¼ cup (30g) custard powder (instant pudding mix)

¼ cup (55g) caster (superfine) sugar

½ teaspoon vanilla extract

1½ cups (375ml) milk

825g (1¾ pounds) canned sliced peaches, drained

2⅓ cups (580ml) thickened (heavy) cream (see notes)

1 Make jelly according to directions on packet; pour into shallow container. Refrigerate 20 minutes or until jelly is almost set.

2 Arrange cake in 3-litre (12-cup) bowl; sprinkle over sherry.

3 Blend custard powder, sugar and extract with a little of the milk in small saucepan; stir in remaining milk. Stir over heat until mixture boils and thickens. Cover surface of custard with plastic wrap; cool.

4 Pour jelly over cake; refrigerate for 15 minutes. Top with peaches. Stir ⅓ cup of the cream into custard; pour over peaches.

5 Whip remaining cream; spread half over custard. Spoon remaining whipped cream into piping bag fitted with large fluted tube; pipe over top of trifle. Refrigerate 3 hours or overnight. Serve trifle topped with maraschino cherries, if you like.

prep + cook time 35 minutes (+ refrigeration & cooling) **serves** 8
nutritional count per serving 31.4g total fat (20.1g saturated fat); 1998kJ (478 cal); 48.7g carbohydrate; 6.4g protein; 1.5g fibre

notes It is fine to use two 300ml (or one 600ml) cartons of cream for this recipe, so as not to waste the remaining 20ml. We used a packaged sponge cake, but you can make your own, if you prefer.

crêpes suzette

¾ cup (110g) plain (all-purpose) flour

3 eggs

2 tablespoons vegetable oil

¾ cup (180ml) milk

orange sauce

125g (4 ounces) unsalted butter

½ cup (110g) caster (superfine) sugar

1½ cups (375ml) orange juice

2 tablespoons lemon juice

⅓ cup (80ml) orange-flavoured liqueur

1 Sift flour into medium bowl, make well in centre; add eggs and oil then gradually whisk in milk until smooth. Pour batter into large jug, cover; stand 1 hour.

2 Heat greased heavy-based crêpe pan or small frying pan; pour ¼ cup of batter into pan, tilting pan to coat base. Cook, over low heat, until browned lightly, loosening edge of crêpe with spatula. Turn crêpe; brown other side. Remove crêpe from pan; cover to keep warm. Repeat with remaining batter to make a total of eight crêpes, greasing pan each time.

3 Make orange sauce.

4 Fold crêpes in half then in half again, place in sauce; warm over low heat.

5 Remove crêpes to serving plates; pour hot sauce over crêpes. Serve with orange slices, if you like.

ORANGE SAUCE Melt butter in large frying pan, add sugar; cook, stirring, until mixture begins to brown. Add strained juices; bring to the boil. Reduce heat; simmer, uncovered, about 3 minutes or until a golden colour. Remove from heat; add liqueur, ignite (see tip).

prep + cook time 1¼ hours (+ standing) **serves** 4
nutritional count per serving
41g total fat
(20.5g saturated fat);
3039kJ (727 cal);
66.9g carbohydrate;
10.3g protein; 1.3g fibre

tip Be very careful when igniting the sauce – use extra long matches, available from supermarkets or camping stores and make sure overhead exhaust fans are turned off. Igniting the sauce burns off the alcohol, leaving a more intense flavour. If you prefer, the sauce can be served as is, without first igniting it.

biscotten torte

24 Milk Coffee biscuits

½ cup (125ml) milk

1½ tablespoons rum

1¼ cup (310ml) thickened (heavy) cream (see note)

almond filling

2 eggs, separated

125g (4 ounces) butter, chopped coarsely, softened

½ cup (110g) caster (superfine) sugar

few drops almond essence

1 cup (120g) ground almonds

½ cup (125ml) milk

1 Make almond filling.

2 Arrange six biscuits lengthways, in two rows of three each, on a large sheet of aluminium foil; brush biscuits generously with combined milk and rum. Spread biscuits with one-third of the almond filling. Repeat layering with remaining biscuits, milk and rum mixture, and almond filling, ending with a layer of biscuits. Wrap torte in foil; refrigerate 8 hours or overnight.

3 Beat cream in small bowl with electric mixer until soft peaks form. Cover torte with cream, running a fork lightly through the cream for a swirled effect. Top with fresh strawberries, if you like.

ALMOND FILLING Beat egg whites in small bowl with electric mixer until soft peaks form. Beat butter, sugar, essence and egg yolks in medium bowl with electric mixer until just combined; do not over-beat. Stir in ground almonds; gradually beat in milk. Fold egg white into almond mixture.

prep time 1 hour (+ refrigeration)
serves 8
nutritional count per serving
42.9g total fat
(22g saturated fat);
2186kJ (523 cal);
38.4g carbohydrate;
8.6g protein; 1.9g fibre

note It is fine to use just the one 300ml carton of cream for this recipe.

sparkling stone fruit and raspberry jelly

½ cup (110g) caster (superfine) sugar

3 cups (750ml) sweet sparkling wine

1½ tablespoons powdered gelatine

½ cup (125ml) water

2 tablespoons lemon juice

1 medium nectarine (170g), sliced thinly

2 medium apricots (100g), sliced thinly

1 medium plum (110g), sliced thinly

200g (6½ ounces) raspberries

1 Stir sugar and 1 cup of the wine in medium saucepan over heat, without boiling, until sugar dissolves; bring to the boil. Reduce heat; simmer, uncovered, without stirring, 5 minutes.

2 Meanwhile, sprinkle gelatine over the water in small heatproof jug. Stand jug in small saucepan of simmering water; stir until gelatine dissolves. Stir gelatine mixture, remaining wine and juice into wine mixture; transfer mixture to heatproof jug.

3 Divide fruit among six 1-cup (250ml) serving glasses. Pour wine mixture over fruit. Cover; refrigerate 3 hours or overnight until firm.

prep + cook time 25 minutes (+ refrigeration) **serves** 6
nutritional count per serving 0.2g total fat (0g saturated fat); 815kJ (195 cal); 25.8g carbohydrate; 3.7g protein; 3g fibre

rice pudding with cardamom and raisins

1 litre (4 cups) milk

1¼ cups (310ml) pouring cream (see notes)

½ cup (110g) caster (superfine) sugar

1 cup (200g) arborio rice

40g (1½ ounces) butter

¼ cup (55g) firmly packed light brown sugar

2 medium apples (300g), peeled, cored, quartered

½ teaspoon each ground cinnamon and cardamom

¾ cup (110g) raisins

1 Stir milk, cream, caster sugar and rice in large saucepan over high heat, without boiling, until sugar dissolves. Bring to the boil; reduce heat. Cook, stirring, about 20 minutes or until rice is tender.
2 Meanwhile, melt butter in small saucepan; stir in brown sugar and apple. Stir over low heat about 10 minutes or until sauce is thickened and apples are caramelised and tender.
3 Stir spices and raisins into rice mixture; cook, stirring, 5 minutes.
4 Serve rice pudding topped with apples.

prep + cook time 40 minutes
serves 4
nutritional count per serving
51g total fat
(33.4g saturated fat);
4193kJ (1003 cal);
120g carbohydrate;
14.1g protein; 2.7g fibre

notes It is fine to use just the one 300ml carton of cream for this recipe.
You can use any dried fruit in place of the raisins in this recipe such as dried apricots or peaches.

cakes

lime buttermilk syrup cake

250g (8 ounces) butter, softened

1 tablespoon grated lime rind

1 cup (220g) caster (superfine) sugar

3 eggs, separated

2 cups (300g) self-raising flour

1 cup (250ml) buttermilk

lime syrup

⅓ cup (80ml) lime juice

¾ cup (165g) caster (superfine) sugar

¼ cup (60ml) water

1 Preheat oven to 180°C/350°F. Grease 20cm (8-inch) baba cake pan (fluted ring pan) well with melted butter; refrigerate or freeze pan to set the butter. Sprinkle a little plain (all-purpose) flour all over the greased area, tap and turn the pan so that all the butter is lightly coated with flour. Turn the pan upside down over the sink or bin and knock out any excess flour.
2 Beat butter, rind and sugar in small bowl with electric mixer until light and fluffy. Beat in egg yolks one at a time.
3 Transfer mixture to large bowl, stir in sifted flour, and buttermilk, in two batches.

4 Beat egg whites in clean small bowl with electric mixer until soft peaks form; fold lightly into cake batter in two batches. Spread mixture into pan.
5 Bake cake about 1 hour. Stand can in pan 5 minutes before turning onto wire rack over tray.
6 Make lime syrup. Pour hot lime syrup evenly over hot cake.

LIME SYRUP Combine ingredients in small saucepan; stir over low heat until sugar is dissolved. Bring to the boil; remove from heat.

prep + cook time 1½ hours **serves** 10
nutritional count per serving
23g total fat (14.4g saturated fat); 1973kJ (472 cal); 61.4g carbohydrate; 6.3g protein; 1.2g fibre

notes When beating the egg whites, wash and dry the beaters from the electric mixer well before using, as any fat or grease will affect the egg whites and you will not get soft peaks. The bowl and the beaters must be completely clean.
Buttermilk makes a deliciously light cake; if unavailable use skim milk. Lime rind and juice give this cake a fresh flavour, but any citrus rind and juice of your choice can be used.

hummingbird cakes with coconut crust

440g (14 ounces) canned crushed pineapple in syrup

1 cup (150g) plain (all-purpose) flour

½ cup (75g) self-raising flour

½ teaspoon bicarbonate of soda (baking soda)

½ teaspoon ground cinnamon

½ teaspoon ground ginger

1 cup (220g) firmly packed light brown sugar

½ cup (40g) desiccated coconut

1 cup mashed banana (300g)

2 eggs, beaten lightly

¾ cup (180ml) vegetable oil

1 teaspoon icing (confectioners') sugar

coconut crust

3 cups (225g) shredded coconut

½ cup (110g) firmly packed light brown sugar

3 eggs, beaten lightly

1 Preheat oven to 180°C/350°F. Line 18 holes of two 12-hole (⅓-cup/80ml) muffin pans with paper cases.
2 Drain pineapple over medium bowl, pressing with spoon to extract as much syrup as possible. Reserve ¼ cup syrup.
3 Sift flours, soda, spices and sugar into large bowl. Stir in drained pineapple, reserved syrup, coconut, banana, egg and oil. Divide mixture into paper cases.
4 Bake cakes 10 minutes.
5 Meanwhile, make coconut crust. Spoon crust over cakes; return to oven, bake a further 15 minutes. Stand cakes in pans 5 minutes before turning, top-side up, onto wire racks to cool. Lightly dust with sifted icing sugar.

COCONUT CRUST Combine ingredients in medium bowl.

prep + cook time 50 minutes
makes 18
nutritional count per cake
10.8g total fat
(2.5g saturated fat);
874kJ (209 cal);
24.8g carbohydrate;
2.5g protein; 1.3g fibre

tip You need two large (460g) over-ripe bananas.

mocha walnut cake

1 cup (220g) caster (superfine) sugar

125g (4 ounces) dark eating (semi-sweet) chocolate, chopped coarsely

1 teaspoon instant coffee granules

2 tablespoons water

125g (4 ounces) unsalted butter, softened

6 eggs, separated

2 cups (250g) finely chopped walnuts

2 tablespoons plain (all-purpose) flour

½ cup (60g) coarsely chopped walnuts, extra

½ cup (125ml) thickened (heavy) cream, whipped

mocha frosting

60g (2 ounces) dark eating (semi-sweet) chocolate, chopped coarsely

90g (3 ounces) unsalted butter, softened

1¼ cups (200g) icing (confectioners') sugar

1 teaspoon instant coffee granules

2 teaspoons hot water

1 Preheat oven to 180°C/350°F. Grease two deep 20cm (8-inch) round cake pans; line bases with baking paper.
2 Combine sugar, chocolate, coffee and the water in small saucepan; stir over low heat, without boiling, until mixture is smooth. Cool.
3 Beat butter in small bowl with electric mixer until pale and creamy; beat in egg yolk, one at a time. Transfer mixture to large bowl; stir in chocolate mixture, finely chopped walnuts and sifted flour.
4 Beat egg whites in medium bowl with electric mixer until soft peaks form. Fold into cake mixture in two batches; pour mixture evenly into pans.
5 Bake cakes about 35 minutes. Stand cakes in pans 5 minutes before turning, top-side up, onto wire racks to cool.
6 Make mocha frosting. Join cold cakes with one-third of the frosting. Spread remaining frosting over top and side of cake. Press coarsely chopped walnuts around side of cake. Fit piping bag with 1½cm (¾-inch) fluted tube; pipe cream around top of cake.

MOCHA FROSTING Melt chocolate in medium heatproof bowl over medium saucepan of simmering water (don't let water touch base of bowl); cool chocolate 10 minutes. Beat butter in small bowl with electric mixer until pale and creamy; gradually beat in sifted icing sugar, chocolate and combined coffee and water.

prep + cook time 1 hour (+ cooling) **serves** 8
nutritional count per serving
65.6g total fat
(27.7g saturated fat);
3781kJ (903 cal);
69.6g carbohydrate;
12.3g protein; 3.7g fibre

rich black forest cake

250g (8 ounces) butter, chopped

1 tablespoon instant coffee granules

1½ cups (375ml) hot water

200g (6½ ounces) dark eating (semi-sweet) chocolate, chopped coarsely

2 cups (440g) caster (superfine) sugar

1½ cups (225g) self-raising flour

1 cup (150g) plain (all-purpose) flour

¼ cup (25g) cocoa powder

2 eggs

2 teaspoons vanilla extract

2⅓ cups (580ml) thickened (heavy) cream (see note)

¼ cup (60ml) cherry-flavoured liqueur

850g (1¾ pounds) canned seeded black cherries, drained, halved

maraschino cherries and chocolate curls to decorate, optional

1 Preheat oven to 150°C/300°F. Grease a deep 23cm (9-inch) round cake pan; line base and side with baking paper.
2 Melt butter in medium saucepan, stir in the combined coffee and hot water, then chocolate and sugar; stir, over low heat, without boiling, until smooth. Transfer mixture to large bowl of electric mixer; cool mixture until just warm.
3 Beat mixture on low speed with electric mixer; gradually beat in sifted flours and cocoa in three batches. Beat in eggs, one at a time, then extract. Pour mixture into pan.
4 Bake cake about 1¾ hours. Stand cake in pan 5 minutes before turning, top-side up, onto wire rack to cool.
5 Beat cream until firm peaks form. Trim top of cake to make it flat. Split cake into three even layers. Place one layer on serving plate, brush with 1 tablespoon of the liqueur; top with a layer of cream and half the cherries. Repeat layer. Brush top layer of cake with remaining liqueur; cover with remaining cream. Decorate with cherries and chocolate curls.

prep + cook time 2¼ hours (+ cooling) **serves** 12
nutritional count per serving
42.3g total fat (28.6g saturated fat); 3039kJ (727 cal); 78.9g carbohydrate; 6.9g protein; 2.7g fibre

note Use a full 600ml carton (tub) of cream instead of wasting the last 20ml.

cinnamon ginger cake with caramel icing

125g (4 ounces) butter, softened

⅓ cup (75g) caster (superfine) sugar

1 egg

¾ cup (265g) golden syrup or treacle

1¾ cups (260g) plain (all-purpose) flour

2 teaspoons ground ginger

1 teaspoon ground cinnamon

½ teaspoon bicarbonate of soda (baking soda)

¾ cup (180ml) hot water

caramel icing

60g (2 ounces) butter, chopped

½ cup (110g) firmly packed light brown sugar

2 tablespoons milk

1½ cups (240g) icing (confectioners') sugar

1 teaspoon vanilla extract

1 Preheat oven to 180°C/350°F. Grease deep 20cm (8-inch) round cake pan.

2 Beat butter and sugar in small bowl with electric mixer until light and fluffy. Beat in egg then gradually add syrup; beat well. Transfer mixture to large bowl, stir in sifted dry ingredients and the water in two batches; stir until smooth. Pour into pan.

3 Bake cake about 1 hour. Stand cake in pan 5 minutes before turning, top-side up, onto wire rack to cool.

4 Make caramel icing. Top cake with icing. Sprinkle with a little extra cinnamon, if you like.

CARAMEL ICING Combine butter and sugar in small saucepan; stir constantly over high heat, without boiling, until butter is melted and sugar dissolved. Add milk; stir a further 2 minutes. Remove from heat: gradually beat in sifted icing sugar and extract.

prep + cook time 1½ hours
serves 8
nutritional count per serving
20.2g total fat (12.9g saturated fat); 2475kJ (592 cal); 101.2g carbohydrate; 4.8g protein; 1.2g fibre

tip To get the decorative effect on the top of the cake; place a paper doily on the cake and sprinkle ground cinnamon over the top. Carefully remove the doily from the top of the cake.

banana cake with passionfruit icing

125g (4 ounces) butter, softened

¾ cup (165g) firmly packed light brown sugar

2 eggs

1½ cups (225g) self-raising flour

½ teaspoon bicarbonate of soda (baking soda)

1 teaspoon mixed spice

1 cup mashed banana (300g)

½ cup (120g) sour cream

¼ cup (60ml) milk

passionfruit icing

1½ cups (240g) icing (confectioners') sugar

1 teaspoon soft butter

2 tablespoons passionfruit pulp, approximately

1 Preheat oven to 180°C/350°F. Grease 15cm x 25cm (6-inch x 10-inch) loaf pan; line base with baking paper.

2 Beat butter and sugar in small bowl with electric mixer until light and fluffy. Beat in eggs, one at a time. Transfer mixture to large bowl; stir in sifted dry ingredients, banana, sour cream and milk. Spread mixture into pan.

3 Bake cake about 50 minutes. Stand cake in pan 5 minutes before turning, top-side up, onto wire rack to cool.

4 Make passionfruit icing. Spread cooled cake with icing.

PASSIONFRUIT ICING Sift icing sugar into medium heatproof bowl; stir in butter and enough pulp to give a firm paste. Stir over medium saucepan of simmering water until icing is of a spreading consistency, taking care not to overheat; use icing immediately.

prep + cook time 1½ hours (+ cooling) **serves** 10
nutritional count per serving
17g total fat (10.7g saturated fat); 1722kJ (412 cal); 61.4g carbohydrate; 4.7g protein; 1.9g fibre

notes You need about two large over-ripe bananas (460g) for this recipe. It is important that the bananas are over-ripe; if they are under-ripe, the cake will be too heavy.

chocolate, apricot and hazelnut cake

1⅔ cups (250g) dried apricots, chopped finely

½ cup (125ml) water

250g (8 ounces) butter, softened

2 cups (440g) firmly packed light brown sugar

6 eggs

1 cup (150g) plain (all-purpose) flour

½ cup (75g) self-raising flour

¼ cup (25g) cocoa powder

1 cup (110g) ground hazelnuts

⅔ cup (160ml) buttermilk

chocolate buttermilk cream

300g (9½ ounces) milk eating chocolate, chopped coarsely

½ cup (125ml) buttermilk

1 cup (160g) icing (confectioners') sugar

1 Combine apricots and the water in small saucepan; bring to the boil. Reduce heat; simmer, covered, stirring occasionally, about 10 minutes or until apricot is soft. Cool.

2 Preheat oven to 160°C/325°F. Grease deep 22cm (8-inch) round cake pan; line base with baking paper.

3 Beat butter and sugar in small bowl with electric mixer until light and fluffy. Beat in eggs, one at a time. Transfer mixture to large bowl; stir in apricot mixture, sifted flours and cocoa, ground hazelnuts and buttermilk, in two batches. Spread mixture into pan.

4 Bake cake about 1¾ hours. Stand cake in pan 10 minutes before turning, top-side up, onto wire rack to cool.

5 Make chocolate buttermilk cream.

6 Split cold cake into three layers; sandwich layers with two-thirds of the chocolate buttermilk cream. Spread top of cake with remaining buttermilk cream. Top with dark chocolate curls. if you like.

CHOCOLATE BUTTERMILK CREAM Stir chocolate and buttermilk in small heatproof bowl over small saucepan of simmering water until smooth; stir in sifted icing sugar. Refrigerate, stirring occasionally, about 30 minutes or until mixture is spreadable.

prep + cook time 2½ hours (+ cooling) **serves** 12
nutritional count per serving
34.5g total fat
(17.8g saturated fat);
2909kJ (696 cal);
87.8g carbohydrate;
10.7g protein; 3.9g fibre

tip To make chocolate curls, run a cheese slicer down the back of a slightly warmed block of chocolate. For smaller curls, run a vegetable peeler down the side of a block of chocolate.

milk chocolate hazelnut whip cupcakes

¼ cup (25g) cocoa powder

¼ cup (60ml) hot water

100g (3½ ounces) dark eating (semi-sweet) chocolate, melted

100g (3½ ounces) butter, melted

1 cup (220g) firmly packed light brown sugar

¾ cup (75g) ground hazelnuts

3 eggs, separated

2 tablespoons chocolate sprinkles

whipped milk chocolate ganache

¾ cup (180ml) pouring cream

315g (10 ounces) milk eating chocolate, chopped coarsely

1 Preheat oven to 180°C/350°F. Line 12-hole (⅓-cup/80ml) muffin pan with paper cases.
2 Blend cocoa with the water in medium bowl until smooth. Stir in chocolate, butter, sugar, ground nuts and egg yolks.
3 Beat egg whites in small bowl with electric mixer until soft peaks form; fold into chocolate mixture in two batches. Fill paper cases three-quarters full.
4 Bake cakes 25 minutes. Stand cakes in pan 5 minutes before turning, top-side up, onto wire rack to cool.
5 Make whipped milk chocolate ganache. Spoon ganache into large piping bag fitted with a large fluted tube. Pipe large swirls of ganache onto cooled cakes. Sprinkle with chocolate sprinkles.

WHIPPED MILK CHOCOLATE GANACHE Bring cream to the boil in small saucepan; remove from heat. When bubbles subside, add chocolate; stir until smooth. Transfer mixture to small bowl. Cover; refrigerate 30 minutes. Beat with an electric mixer until light and fluffy.

prep + cook time 50 minutes (+ cooling & refrigeration)
makes 12
nutritional count per cake
29.7g total fat
(17g saturated fat);
1857kJ (444 cal);
40.8g carbohydrate;
5.3g protein; 1.3g fibre

baked delights

choc brownies with sour cream frosting

125g (4 ounces) butter, chopped

185g (6 ounces) dark eating (semi-sweet) chocolate, chopped coarsely

1 cup (220g) caster (superfine) sugar

2 teaspoons vanilla extract

2 eggs, beaten lightly

1 cup (150g) plain (all-purpose) flour

½ cup (60g) coarsely chopped pecans

sour cream frosting

100g (3 ounces) dark eating (semi-sweet) chocolate, chopped coarsely

¼ cup (60g) sour cream

1 Preheat oven to 180°C/350°F. Grease deep 19cm (8-inch) square cake pan; line base with baking paper.

2 Place butter and chocolate in small saucepan; stir over low heat until melted. Transfer mixture to large bowl. Stir in sugar and extract, then eggs, sifted flour and nuts. Pour mixture into pan.

3 Bake about 30 minutes or until set; cool brownie in pan.

4 Make sour cream frosting. Turn brownie out of pan; spread top with frosting. Refrigerate until set before cutting.

SOUR CREAM FROSTING Melt chocolate in small heatproof bowl over small saucepan of simmering water. Stir in sour cream; stir constantly until mixture is smooth and glossy.

prep + cook time 55 minutes (+ cooling & refrigeration) **makes** 16
nutritional count per piece
16.8g total fat (10.5g saturated fat); 1187kJ (284 cal); 31g carbohydrate; 3.1g protein; 1.5g fibre

vanilla passionfruit slice

1 sheet puff pastry

¼ cup (55g) caster (superfine) sugar

¼ cup (35g) cornflour (cornstarch)

1½ tablespoons custard powder (instant pudding mix)

1¼ cups (310ml) milk

30g (1 ounce) butter

1 egg yolk

½ teaspoon vanilla extract

passionfruit icing

¾ cup (120g) icing (confectioners') sugar

1 tablespoon passionfruit pulp

1 teaspoon water, approximately

1 Preheat oven to 240°C/475°F. Grease 8cm x 26cm (3¼-inch x 10½-inch) bar cake pan; line with strip of foil extending over long sides of pan.

2 Place pastry sheet on oven tray. Bake about 15 minutes or until puffed; cool. Split pastry in half horizontally; remove and discard any uncooked pastry from centre. Flatten pastry pieces gently with hand; trim both to fit bar pan. Place top half of pastry in pan, top-side down.

3 Meanwhile, combine sugar, cornflour and custard powder in medium saucepan; gradually stir in milk. Stir over high heat until mixture boils and thickens. Reduce heat; simmer, stirring, about 3 minutes or until custard is thick and smooth. Remove pan from heat; stir in butter, egg yolk and extract.

4 Spread hot custard over the pastry in pan; top with remaining pastry, bottom-side up, press down gently. Cool to room temperature.

5 Meanwhile, make passionfruit icing.

6 Spread icing over pastry; set at room temperature. Refrigerate 3 hours before cutting.

PASSIONFRUIT ICING Sift icing sugar into small heatproof bowl; stir in passionfruit and enough water to make a thick paste. Stir over small saucepan of simmering water until icing is spreadable.

prep + cook time 45 minutes (+ cooling & refrigeration)
makes 8
nutritional count per slice
10.1g total fat
(3.6g saturated fat);
1028kJ (246 cal);
36.7g carbohydrate;
3g protein; 0.7g fibre

chelsea buns

4 teaspoons (14g) dry yeast

1 teaspoon caster (superfine) sugar

3 cups (560g) plain (all-purpose) flour

1½ cups (375ml) warm milk

½ teaspoon ground cinnamon

¼ teaspoon ground nutmeg

½ teaspoon mixed spice

2 teaspoons grated orange rind

1 tablespoon caster (superfine) sugar, extra

1 egg, beaten lightly

45g (1½ ounces) butter, melted

15g (½ ounce) butter, melted, extra

2 tablespoons raspberry jam (conserve)

½ cup (75g) dried currants

¼ cup (55g) firmly packed light brown sugar

½ cup (60g) coarsely chopped roasted pecans

3 teaspoons warmed honey

coffee icing

1½ cups (240g) icing (confectioners') sugar

15g (½ ounce) butter, melted

2 tablespoons warm milk

3 teaspoons instant coffee granules

1 Combine yeast, caster sugar, 1 tablespoon of the flour, and warm milk in a small bowl. Cover; stand in warm place about 10 minutes or until frothy.
2 Combine remaining sifted flour, spices, rind and extra caster sugar in large bowl, stir in egg, butter and yeast mixture; mix to a soft dough. Knead dough on floured surface about 10 minutes or until smooth and elastic. Place dough in large greased bowl. Cover; stand in warm place about 1 hour or until doubled in size.
3 Grease two deep 22cm (9-inch) round cake pans.
4 Turn dough onto floured surface; knead 1 minute. Roll dough into 23cm x 36cm (9-inch x 14½-inch) rectangle. Brush dough with extra melted butter, spread with jam. Sprinkle dough with combined currants, brown sugar and nuts, leaving a 2cm (1-inch) border all around.
5 Roll dough up firmly from long side like a swiss roll. Cut dough evenly into 12 pieces; place six pieces, cut-side up, in each pan. Cover, stand in a warm place about 30 minutes or until buns have risen slightly.
6 Meanwhile, preheat oven to 200°C/ 400°F.
7 Bake buns about 30 minutes or until golden brown.
8 Make coffee icing. Turn buns, top-side up, onto wire rack. Brush hot buns with honey, drizzle with coffee icing; cool.

COFFEE ICING Sift icing sugar into small bowl; stir in butter, milk and coffee until smooth.

prep + cook time 1½ hours (+ standing) **makes** 12
nutritional count per piece
11.2g total fat
(4.7g saturated fat);
1726kJ (413 cal);
70.3g carbohydrate;
8g protein; 2.7g fibre

frangipane jam drops

raspberry coconut slice

90g (3 ounces) butter, softened

½ cup (110g) caster (superfine) sugar

1 egg

⅓ cup (50g) self-raising flour

⅔ cup (100g) plain (all-purpose) flour

½ cup (160g) raspberry jam (conserve)

coconut topping

2 eggs

⅓ cup (75g) caster (superfine) sugar

2 cups (160g) desiccated coconut

1 Preheat oven to 180°C/350°F. Grease 19cm x 29cm (7½-inch x 11½-inch) slice pan; line with baking paper, extending paper 5cm (2-inches) over long sides.
2 Beat butter, sugar and egg in small bowl with electric mixer until light and fluffy; stir in sifted flours in two batches. Spread mixture over base of pan. Spread jam evenly over top.
3 Make coconut topping. Spread topping over top of jam.
4 Bake about 35 minutes. Cool in pan; cut when cold.

COCONUT TOPPING Beat eggs lightly with fork in medium bowl; stir in sugar and coconut.

prep + cook time 50 minutes
makes 18
nutritional count per piece
10.8g total fat
(7.6g saturated fat);
831kJ (198 cal);
22.8g carbohydrate;
2.5g protein; 1.8g fibre

variation Substitute raspberry jam with apricot jam, and use 1 cup of coconut and 1 cup ground almonds instead of 2 cups coconut.

frangipane jam drops

125g (4 ounces) butter, softened

½ teaspoon vanilla extract

½ cup (110g) caster (superfine) sugar

1 cup (120g) ground almonds

1 egg

⅔ cup (100g) plain (all-purpose) flour

2 tablespoons raspberry jam (conserve)

1 Preheat oven to 180°C/350°F. Line two oven trays with baking paper.
2 Beat butter, extract, sugar and almonds in small bowl with electric mixer until light and fluffy. Add egg, beat until just combined; stir in sifted flour.

3 Drop level tablespoons of mixture onto trays 5cm (2-inches) apart. Use handle of a wooden spoon to make a small hole about 1cm (½-inch) deep in the top of each biscuit. Fill holes with ¼ teaspoon jam.
4 Bake biscuits about 15 minutes; cool on trays.

prep + cook time 40 minutes
makes 24
nutritional count per biscuit
7.3g total fat
(3.1g saturated fat);
456kJ (109 cal);
9.3g carbohydrate;
1.8g protein; 0.6g fibre

raspberry coconut slice

cooking techniques

To toast pistachios, stir nuts over a low heat in a dry frying pan until golden brown. Remove the nuts immediately from the pan to stop them from burning.

To zest citrus fruit A zester has very small, and very sharp, holes that cut the rind (the outermost layer of the fruit) into thin ribbons, but leaves the bitter pith behind.

To melt chocolate, place chopped chocolate into a heatproof bowl over a pan of simmering water. The water mustn't touch the base of the bowl. Stir until smooth, and remove as soon as it's melted.

To make simple chocolate curls, have the chocolate at room temperature and drag a vegetable peeler, down the long side to make small curls.

To rest the pastry, pat the dough into a flat shape, this makes it easier to roll out later, and wrap it in a piece of plastic wrap; refrigerate it for about 30 minutes – if the dough is too hard to roll out after refrigeration, let it stand a bit before rolling.

To roll out pastry, place it between sheets of baking or greaseproof paper, and roll from the centre to the edge, without rolling over the edge. Always roll from the centre out – roll from the centre up, then the centre down, give a quarter turn and roll again. This helps to roll out the pastry evenly, and to keep its rounded shape.

To cover the top of a pie, first brush the edge of the pastry in the dish with a little water. Roll the pastry lid out to about 5cm larger than the top of the dish; gently roll the pastry around the rolling pin and unroll it over the filling, making sure it completely covers the top of the pie dish.

To trim the pastry, hold the pie dish flat on the palm of one hand, then use a sharp knife to make a downward cutting action, and trim away the excess pastry at a 45° angle.

To grease a bundt pan, use a pastry brush to thickly grease the pan with soft butter. Sprinkle the pan with a little flour then tap out the excess flour.

To split a cake into even layers (1), use bamboo skewers as a guide for the knife as you split the cake. For large cakes, push long skewers through the cake; for small cakes, use toothpicks to mark the layer.

To split a cake into even layers (2), Use a sharp serrated knife to split the cake. Cut the cake barely above the skewers, you should feel the knife touch the skewers as you cut through the cake.

Hull a strawberry The hull, or calyx, is the green leafy top. Cut around the leafy top and into the pale flesh underneath, and discard. Wash and drain the strawberries before using.

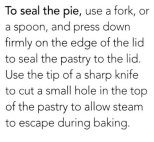

To seal the pie, use a fork, or a spoon, and press down firmly on the edge of the lid to seal the pastry to the lid. Use the tip of a sharp knife to cut a small hole in the top of the pastry to allow steam to escape during baking.

To neatly cover the side of a cake, cover the side only with frosting, butter cream or icing. Spread coconut, nuts (or whatever covering is to be used) in a large flat pan and, holding the cake like a wheel, roll the side of the cake until it is evenly covered.

To rub butter into flour, chop the chilled butter into cubes, and use your fingertips (the coolest part of your hands) to squash butter cubes through the flour. Do this quickly to keep the butter cold. Shake the bowl so any large lumps come to the surface. The mixture should end up like breadcrumbs.

To grate a lime, use the small holes on a grater, finely grate the rind, ensuring only the rind is grated, and not the bitter white pith underneath. Rasp graters (thin metal graters), such as a Microplane grater, can also be used.

glossary

ALMONDS flat, pointy-ended nuts with a pitted brown shell enclosing a creamy white kernel that is covered by a brown skin.
ground also known as almond meal; nuts are powdered to a coarse flour-like texture.

ARBORIO RICE small, round-grain rice, well-suited to absorb a large amount of liquid; especially suitable for risottos.

ANGOSTURA BITTERS brand-name of a type of aromatic bitters; used mainly in drinks, from aperitifs and cocktails to digestifs. Its recipe is a closely guarded secret, but it is made of many herbs and spices.

ARROWROOT a starch made from the rhizome of a Central American plant; used mostly for thickening. Cornflour can be substituted but will not give as clear a glaze.

BACON SLICES also known as bacon rashers; made from cured and smoked pork side.

BASIL an aromatic herb; there are many types, but the most commonly used is sweet, or common, basil.

BAY LEAVES aromatic leaves from the bay tree used to flavour soups, stocks and casseroles.

BEEF
fillet a generic name given to a steak cut from the beef tenderloin.
silverside also known as topside roast; used for making corned beef, usually sold vacuum-sealed in brine.

BICARBONATE OF SODA also known as baking or carb soda; a mild alkali used as a raising agent in baking.

BISCUITS also known as cookies.
milk coffee an uniced, plain biscuit sweetened with golden syrup.

BREADCRUMBS
packaged fine-textured, crunchy, purchased white breadcrumbs.
stale one- or two-day-old bread made into crumbs by blending or processing.

BUTTER use salted or unsalted (sweet) butter; 125g is equal to one stick (4 ounces) of butter.

BUTTON MUSHROOMS small, cultivated white mushrooms with a mild flavour.

BUTTERMILK originally the term given to the slightly sour liquid left after butter was churned from cream, today it is commercially made similarly to yogurt. Sold alongside all fresh milk products in supermarkets; despite the implication of its name, it is low in fat.

CARDAMOM can be purchased in pod, seed or ground form. Has a distinctive aromatic, sweetly rich flavour and is one of the world's most expensive spices.

CHEESE
goat's made from goat's milk; has an earthy, strong taste. Available in both soft and firm textures, in various shapes and sizes, sometimes rolled in ash or herbs.
gouda mild cream-coloured Dutch cheese made from cow's milk. Has a mild nutty flavour. Shaped in rounds.

CHERRY-FLAVOURED LIQUEUR we used Kirsch, but you can use your favourite brand.

CHICKEN
breast fillet the breast is halved, then skinned and boned.
tenderloin thin strip of meat lying just under the breast, especially good for stir-frying.
thigh fillet has the skin and centre bone removed.

CHILLI available in many different types and sizes. Use rubber gloves when seeding and chopping fresh chillies as they can burn your skin. Removing seeds and membranes lessens the heat level.
cayenne pepper a long, thin-fleshed, extremely hot red chilli usually sold dried and ground.
jalapeño fairly hot green chillies, available bottled in brine or fresh from specialty greengrocers; we used the medium-hot, sweetish chopped bottled version in our recipes.
long red available both fresh and dried; a generic term used for any moderately hot, long, thin chilli (about 6cm to 8cm long).

powder the Asian variety, made from dried ground thai chillies, is the hottest; it can be used as a substitute for fresh chillies in the proportion of ½ teaspoon ground chilli powder to 1 medium chopped fresh chilli.

CINNAMON dried inner bark of the shoots of the cinnamon tree; available in stick (quill) or ground form.

COCOA POWDER also known as cocoa; dried, unsweetened, roasted then ground cocoa beans (cacao seeds).

COCONUT
desiccated unsweetened coconut that's been concentrated, dried, then very finely shredded.
flaked dried, flaked, coconut flesh.
shredded thin strips of dried coconut.

CORIANDER both the stems and roots of coriander are used in Thai cooking; wash well before using. Also available ground or as seeds; these should not be substituted for fresh coriander as the tastes are completely different.

CORNFLOUR (cornstarch) used as a thickening agent. Available as 100% maize (corn) and wheaten cornflour. Wheaten cornflour is made from wheat rather than corn and gives sponge cakes a lighter texture (due to the fact that wheaten cornflour has some gluten).

CREAM OF TARTAR the acid ingredient in baking powder; added to confectionery mixtures to help prevent sugar from crystallising. Keeps frostings creamy and improves volume when beating egg whites.

CREAM we use fresh cream, also known as pure, pouring or single cream, with a minimum fat content of 35%, unless otherwise stated. It has no additives, unlike commercially thickened cream.
sour a thick cultured soured cream. Minimum fat content 35%.
thickened a whipping cream containing a thickener. Minimum fat content 35%.

CREAMING SODA a carbonated, sweet-tasting soft drink; may contain vanilla and/or other flavourings and colourings.

CURRY POWDER a blend of ground spices used for convenience when making Indian/Asian food. Choose mild or hot to suit your taste, heat tolerance and the recipe.

CUSTARD POWDER MIXTURE used to make pouring custard; similar to North American instant pudding mixes.

DILL also known as dill weed; used fresh or dried, in seed form or ground. Has a sweet anise/celery flavour. Its distinctive feathery, frond-like fresh leaves are grassier and more subtle than the dried version or the seeds.

DILL PICKLE a small cucumber that's preserved in brine or vinegar flavoured with dill seed.

EGG some recipes in this book may call for raw or barely cooked eggs; exercise caution if there is a salmonella problem in your area.

FLAT-LEAF PARSLEY also known as continental or italian parsley

FLOUR
plain a general all-purpose flour made from wheat.
self-raising plain flour sifted with baking powder in the proportion of 1 cup flour to 2 teaspoons baking powder. Also known as self-rising.

FOOD COLOURING dyes that can be used to change the colour of various foods. These dyes can be eaten and do not change the taste to a noticeable extent.

FRENCH-TRIMMED also sometimes just seen as 'frenched'; a butchers' term referring to a cutting method where all excess sinew, gristle and fat from the bone end of meat cutlets, racks or shanks are removed and the bones scraped clean.

GELATINE we used powdered gelatine. It is also available in sheet form, known as leaf gelatine.

GIN is a clear spirit based on barley and rye to which a mix of selected herbs and spices are added. These flavourings, known as 'botanicals', include aniseed, coriander, fruit peels and juniper berry.

GINGER, GROUND also known as powdered ginger; used as a flavouring in cakes, pies and puddings but can't be substituted for fresh ginger.

GOLDEN SYRUP a by-product of refined sugar cane; pure maple syrup or honey can be substituted. Treacle is a thick, dark syrup not unlike molasses; a by-product of sugar refining.

HAMBURGER BUNS soft, white, round rolls originally named as they were used to sandwich hamburger patties.

HAZELNUTS, GROUND also known as hazelnut meal.

HUNDREDS AND THOUSANDS (nonpareils) tiny sugar-syrup-coated sugar crystals that come in a variety of bright colours and are used to decorate cakes and party foods.

JELLY CRYSTALS a powdered mixture of gelatine, sweetener and artificial fruit flavouring that's used to make a moulded, translucent, quivering dessert. Also known as jello.

KECAP MANIS, see sauces.

KITCHEN STRING made of a natural product, such as cotton or hemp, so that it neither affects the flavour of the food it's tied around nor melts when heated.

LAMB
backstrap also known as eye of loin; the larger fillet from the loin (before it's cut into loin chops or cutlets).
cutlet small, tender rib chop.
fillet also known as lamb tenderloin. From the loin (lower back) section.

MAYONNAISE a rich, creamy dressing made with egg yolks, vegetable oil, mustard and vinegar or lemon juice. We use whole-egg mayonnaise in our recipes unless otherwise specified.

MINT LEAVES a herb that includes many varieties including spearmint, common mint and peppermint. Spearmint has long, smooth leaves, and is the one that greengrocers sell, while common mint, with rounded, pebbly leaves, is the one that most people grow. Spearmint has the stronger flavour.

MIXED HERBS a dried commercial blend of crushed thyme, rosemary, basil, marjoram, oregano and sage; available in supermarkets.

MIXED SPICE a blend of ground spices usually consisting of allspice, cinnamon and nutmeg.

MUDDLER a bartender's tool, used to crush, or mash, fruits, herbs and/ or spices in the bottom of a glass to release their flavour.

MUSTARD
american-style bright yellow in colour, a sweet mustard containing mustard seeds, sugar, salt, spices and garlic. Serve with hot dogs and hamburgers.
dijon a distinctively flavoured, pale brown, mild tasting french mustard.
powder finely ground white (yellow) mustard seeds.
wholegrain also known as seeded. A French-style coarse-grain mustard made from crushed mustard seeds and dijon-style french mustard.

NUTMEG the dried nut of an evergreen tree native to Indonesia; it is available in ground form or you can grate your own with a fine grater.

OIL
cooking spray we use a cholesterol-free spray made from canola oil.
olive made from ripened olives. Extra virgin and virgin are the best, while extra light or light refers to taste not fat levels.
vegetable sourced from plants.

OLIVE, GREEN those harvested before fully ripened and are, as a rule, denser and more bitter than their black relatives.

ORANGE-FLAVOURED LIQUEUR We use Grand Marnier, which is based on cognac; use your favourite brand.

OREGANO a herb, also known as wild marjoram; has a woody stalk with clumps of tiny, dark green leaves that have a pungent, peppery flavour and are used fresh or dried.

PAPRIKA ground dried sweet red capsicum (bell pepper); there are many grades and types available, including sweet, hot, mild and smoked.

PASTRY

puff a crisp, light, layered pastry; layers of dough and margarine are folded and rolled many times making many layers. When baked, it becomes a high, crisp, flaky pastry.

shortcrust is a tender, crunchy, melt in the mouth buttery pastry. Once baked it is a light, crumbly, easily broken short pastry.

PORK LOIN from the loin section that runs across most of the back.

PORT fortified wine (wine to which additional alcohol has been added, most commonly in the form of brandy, which is a spirit distilled from wine).

POTATOES, BABY NEW also known as chats; not a separate variety but an early harvest with very thin skin; can be used unpeeled.

RAISINS dried sweet grapes.

REDCURRANT JELLY a preserve made from redcurrants; used as a glaze for desserts and meats, or in sauces.

ROGAN JOSH a curry paste of medium heat, from the Kashmir region of India. Made from fresh chillies or paprika, tomato and spices, especially cardamom.

ROSEWATER distilled from rose petals, and used in the Middle East, North Africa, and India to flavour desserts. Don't confuse this with rose essence, which is more concentrated.

SAGE a pungent herb with narrow, grey-green leaves; slightly bitter with a slightly musty mint aroma. Dried sage comes whole, crumbled or ground. It should be stored in a cool, dark place for no more than three months.

SALT

cooking coarser than table salt, but not as large-flaked as sea salt: it is sold packaged in bags in most supermarkets.

flakes reminiscent of snowflakes. Sea water is evaporated producing a salt brine that's fed into an open evaporating pan. The brine is slowly heated until delicate pyramid-shaped crystals of salt appear. The finished product is light, flaky sea salt.

table the common salt normally found on every table. It is a finely ground, refined rock salt with some additives to keep it free-flowing. Most table salt is available either plain or iodised.

SAUCES

cranberry a packaged product made of cranberries cooked in sugar syrup; has an astringent flavour.

Tabasco brand name of an extremely fiery sauce made from vinegar, hot red chillies and salt.

tomato also known as ketchup or catsup; a flavoured condiment made from tomatoes, vinegar and spices.

kecap manis a dark, thick sweet soy sauce. Depending on the brand, the soy's sweetness is derived from the addition of either molasses or palm sugar when brewed.

worcestershire a dark coloured condiment made from soy sauce, garlic, tamarind, onions, molasses, lime, anchovies, vinegar and various other seasonings.

SHALLOTS also called french shallots, golden shallots or eschalots.

SUGAR

brown a soft, fine sugar retaining molasses. Dark brown sugar may be substituted.

caster also known as superfine or finely granulated table sugar.

icing sugar also known as confectioners' or powdered sugar; granulated sugar crushed together with a small amount of cornflour.

white a coarse, granulated table sugar, also known as crystal sugar.

SWEET SHERRY a fortified wine that can be consumed or used in cooking.

SWEET SPARKLING WINE once known as champagne, though, legally, this term now only refers to sparkling wine from the northeast region of Champagne in France.

THYME a member of the mint family. The 'household' variety, simply called thyme in most shops, is French thyme; it has tiny grey-green leaves that give off a pungent minty, light-lemon aroma. Dried thyme comes in both leaf and powdered form.

TOMATO

cherry also known as tiny tim or tom thumb tomatoes; small and round.

paste triple-concentrated tomato puree used to flavour soups, stews, sauces and casseroles.

TORTILLAS thin, round unleavened bread originating in Mexico. Two kinds are available, one made from wheat flour and the other from corn.

VANILLA EXTRACT is made by extracting the flavour from the vanilla bean pod; the pods are soaked, usually in alcohol, to capture the authentic flavour. Vanilla essence is not a suitable substitute.

VERJUICE is unfermented grape juice with a fresh lemony-vinegar flavour. It's available in supermarkets, usually in the vinegar section.

VERMOUTH a white wine that has been steeped with an infusion of herbs, plants, roots, leaves, peels, seed and flowers.

VINEGAR

balsamic originally from Modena, Italy, there are now many balsamic vinegars on the market ranging in pungency and quality depending on how long they have been aged. Quality can be determined up to a point by price; use the most expensive sparingly. Made from the juice of Trebbiano grapes; it is a deep rich brown colour with a sweet and sour flavour.

brown malt made from fermented malt and beech shavings.

red wine based on fermented red wine.

rice a colourless vinegar made from fermented rice and flavoured with sugar and salt. Also known as seasoned rice vinegar.

white made from spirit of cane sugar.

VODKA distilled from a fermented mash of grain, which is distilled to remove all flavour. Made mainly from corn, rye and wheat, and occasionally from potatoes.

YEAST a 7g (¼oz) sachet of dried yeast (2 teaspoons) is equal to 15g (½oz) compressed yeast if substituting one for the other.

V - vegetarian

index

Published in 2012 by ACP Books, Sydney
ACP Books are published by ACP Magazines Limited
a division of Nine Entertainment Co.
54 Park St, Sydney
GPO Box 4088, Sydney, NSW 2001.
phone (02) 9282 8618; fax (02) 9126 3702
acpbooks@acpmagazines.com.au; www.acpbooks.com.au

ACP BOOKS
Publishing Director, ACP Magazines · Gerry Reynolds
Publisher · Sally Wright
Editorial and Food Director · Pamela Clark
Creative Director · Hieu Chi Nguyen

Published and Distributed in the United Kingdom by Octopus Publishing Group
Endeavour House
189 Shaftesbury Avenue
London WC2H 8JY
United Kingdom
phone (+44)(0)207 632 5400; fax (+44)(0)207 632 5405
info@octopus-publishing.co.uk;
www.octopusbooks.co.uk

Printed by Toppan Printing Co., China

International foreign language rights, Brian Cearnes, ACP Books bcearnes@acpmagazines.com.au

A catalogue record for this book is available from the British Library.
ISBN: 978-1-74245-320-0 (pbk.)
© ACP Magazines Ltd 2012
ABN 18 053 273 546

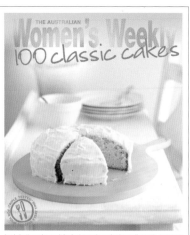

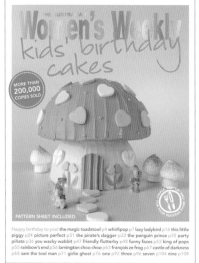
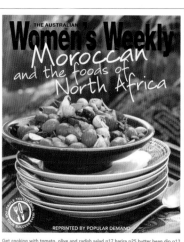

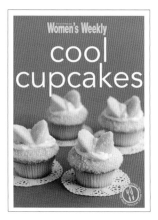